# YANKEE'S
## FAVORITE RECIPES:
### Over 100 of the Finest Recipes
### From YANKEE Magazine!

# TABLE OF CONTENTS:

# INTRODUCTION

We've published dozens of cookbooks over the course of the fifty-five years since *Yankee* began. And yet this simple collection could well be the best of them all. True, there are no fancy color photographs, illustrations, or lavish designs. But the recipes in this little volume represent the very favorite recipes of *Yankee*'s editors, staff members, and writers. Taken from past issues (mostly from the on-going Great New England cooks series), they're the ones each of us remembers and likes above all the others.

The "favorites" I submitted? Well I tended toward the New England "traditionals" — Veal Chops Braised in Cider, Mildred's Fish Chowder, Scalloped Oysters Cormier, and Bow' Lobster Pie. Oh, yes — Shaker Raised Squash Biscuits. Makes my cheeks ache just to think about them.

My wife, Sally, listed mostly desserts as her favorites. Like the Cider Sherbert, the Rhubarb Crunch, the Apple Crumb Pie, and the Gram White's Soft Ginger Cookies, originally submitted to *Yankee* in 1985 by the Groton, Vermont, Community Club. "These are all real classics," she said.

So all I can say now is that if the recipes in the future issues of *Yankee* can stand up to these from the past (and I have good reason to believe they will!), well, we'll just all have to go out and buy new clothes . . .

Judson D. Hale, Sr.
Editor, Yankee Magazine

# CONVENTIONS, ABBREVIATIONS & EQUIVALENTS

## CONVENTIONS

**Butter** — Wherever butter is called for in a recipe, either butter *or* oleomargarine can be used with equal success. Butter is expensive, oleomargarine more reasonable; there is a slight taste difference — no question, butter *is* better. But if, like the Editor, you have gotten used to margarine, use it by all means.

**Flour** — Unless otherwise specified in the recipe, "flour" means all-purpose white flour.

**Herbs** — These are dried unless fresh are specifically required.

**Oil, cooking or Salad** — In all recipes except those for Salads, "cooking oil" means liquid corn, safflower, or other vegetable oil, but *not* olive oil. "Salad oil" means your favorite kind — including olive oil.

**Shortening** — When a recipe calls for *shortening,* solid vegetable shortening such as "Crisco" is meant. Do not use cooking oil, lard, or bacon fat. In a pinch, oleomargarine can be used, as it, too, is solid vegetable shortening, but it is salted, and does have a slightly different taste.

**Sour Cream** — Where this is called for, the commercial product is meant, not cream soured in your refrigerator.

**Spices** — These are ground unless whole cloves, crystalline ginger, or stick cinnamon is specified.

**Whipped Salad Dressing** — A Miracle-Whip-type product.

**Sugar** — "Sugar" is always white granulated sugar; confectioners' sugar and brown sugar are so specified. Where both brown and white sugars are called for, white granulated sugar is referred to as "white sugar." Brown sugar measurements are for packed amounts.

**Baking, Beating, or Blending times** — These may vary slightly with different ovens, beaters, or blenders.

**Can Sizes** — Sizes vary slightly with different brands, but similar-size cans usually are similar in content. All can sizes given are based on popular brands with national distribution.

**Oven Heat** — Best results are always achieved by preheating the oven to the temperature required in the recipe. Please read recipe through before you begin to mix ingredients and *preheat oven* to specified temperature.

## ABBREVIATIONS

| | |
|---|---|
| teaspoon(s) | t. (1 t. or 2 t.) |
| tablespoon(s) | T. (1 T. or 2 T.) |
| pound(s) | lb(s). |
| ounce(s) | oz. |
| package(s) | pkg(s). |
| pint(s) | pt(s). |
| quart(s) | qt(s). |
| gallon(s) | gal(s). |
| degrees Fahrenheit | °F. |
| inch(es) | " — (9" by 13" pan) |

## EQUIVALENTS

| | |
|---|---|
| pinch or dash | less than 1/8 teaspoon |
| 3 teaspoons | 1 tablespoon |
| 2 tablespoons | 1 liquid ounce |
| 4 tablespoons | 1/4 cup |
| 8 tablespoons | 1/2 cup |
| 16 tablespoons | 1 cup |
| 1 cup | 1 gill |
| 2 cups | 1 pint |
| 4 pints | 1 quart |
| 4 quarts | 1 gallon |
| 2 cups liquid | 1 pound |
| 2 cups butter | 1 pound |
| 2 cups granulated sugar | 1 pound |
| 4 cups flour | 1 pound |
| chocolate, 1 square unsweetened | 1 ounce |
| 4 cups grated cheese | 1 pound |
| 8 egg whites | 1 cup (approx.) |
| 16 egg yolks | 1 cup (approx.) |
| juice of 1 lemon | 2 to 3 tablespoons |
| 1 cup raw macaroni | 2 cups cooked |
| 1 cup raw rice | 3 to 4 cups cooked |
| 1 cup whipping cream | 2 to 2-1/2 cups whipped cream |

# MEATS

## MOUSSAKA

2 medium eggplants
cooking oil
1-1/2 lbs. ground meat
  (lamb or beef)
1 cup chopped onion
1/2 cup burgundy wine
2 T. dried parsley
5 T. tomato paste
1/3 cup water
1/2 t. salt
1/4 t. pepper
1 cup grated Cheddar
  cheese
1 cup fine bread crumbs
4 eggs
1/4 t. cinnamon
6 T. butter
1/2 cup flour
3 cups milk
1/2 t. salt
1/4 t. pepper
1/4 t. nutmeg
paprika

Slice the eggplant into 1/2-inch thick slices, sprinkle with salt, and set aside. Heat the cooking oil in a large skillet and brown the meat and the onion, then drain off the fat. Add to the skillet the wine, parsley, tomato paste, water, salt, and pepper, and simmer slowly, stirring often, until the liquid is nearly all absorbed. Remove from heat and add 1/2 cup of the cheese, 1/2 cup of the bread crumbs, 2 of the eggs (well beaten), and the cinnamon. Set the mixture aside. In a saucepan, melt the butter, whisk in the flour, then slowly whisk in the milk. Put over low heat, stirring often, until the mixture thickens. Mix a small amount of this sauce into 2 beaten eggs then pour this combination back into the sauce. Add the salt, pepper, and nutmeg, and cook, stirring, for 2 more minutes on low heat.

In a frying pan with 1/4 inch oil, lightly brown the eggplant slices on both sides. Sprinkle the remaining 1/2 cup bread crumbs on the bottom of a 9" by 13" baking dish and arrange half of the eggplant slices in a layer over the crumbs. Spread the meat mixture over the eggplant, and then arrange the rest of the eggplant over the meat. Pour the cream sauce over the top, and sprinkle with the remaining cheese and paprika. Bake uncovered at 375°F. for 40 minutes, then let stand 10 minutes before serving. *Serves 6 generously.*

## RACK OR CROWN ROAST OF LAMB

Brush meat with olive oil and roast at 400°F. for 20 minutes. Brush mustard on meat. Mix crumbs with garlic, parsley, rosemary, pepper, and thyme, and gently apply a coating by hand over the mustard. Continue to roast at 375°F. for 25 to 35 minutes (lamb will be pink inside at 25 minutes). Serve with a mustard or garlic hollandaise sauce, if desired.

1 rack or crown of lamb (about 3 to 5 lbs.)
olive oil
Dijon mustard
1 cup fresh bread crumbs; or ground almonds or macadamia nuts
2 garlic cloves, minced
1/4 cup minced parsley
1/4 t. rosemary, crushed
1/2 t. pepper
1/4 t. thyme

## LAMB SALAD

In a small bowl combine oil, vinegar, lemon juice, mustard, oregano, salt, hot pepper sauce, and garlic. In a large bowl combine lamb, broccoli, mushrooms, and peppers. Toss lamb and vegetables with dressing. Serve on a bed of lettuce and sprinkle with chopped basil or parsley. *Serves 4.*

**Note:** Other vegetables may be added as desired, including blanched, julienned carrots, sliced or julienned zucchini or yellow squash, tomato wedges, steamed brussels sprouts.

2/3 cup olive oil or vegetable oil
1/4 cup red wine vinegar
1 T. freshly squeezed lemon juice
2 t. Dijon-style mustard
3/4 t. dried oregano, crumbled
1/4 t. salt
3 drops hot pepper sauce
1 clove garlic, peeled and minced
2 cups cooked, cubed lamb
1 bunch broccoli, cut into flowerets
1/2 lb. (about 3 cups) mushrooms, sliced
2 small red sweet peppers, seeded and cut into strips
leaf lettuce
chopped basil or parsley

## BOEUF ABDULLAH *(Lebanese Meatballs)*

1/2 cup chopped onion
3 T. butter
1 lb. ground beef
1 egg, beaten
2 slices bread soaked in
 1/2 cup milk
1 t. salt
1/8 t. pepper
1 cup dry bread crumbs
2 cups plain yogurt

Sauté onion in 1 tablespoon butter until transparent. Cool slightly. Mix with meat, egg, bread, and seasonings. Shape into 1-1/4 inch balls and roll them in dry bread crumbs. Brown slowly in remaining 2 tablespoons butter. Drain off all but 2 tablespoons fat. Gently spoon yogurt over and around meatballs. Simmer for 20 minutes. Serve hot with rice or wheat pilaf. For extra flavor dissolve a bouillon cube in the water used to cook the rice. *Serves 6-8.*

## BEEF SAUSAGE

2 lbs. hamburger (top
 grade)
1 cup bread crumbs
1/2 cup water
1-1/2 t. salt
1 t. nutmeg
1 t. black pepper
2 t. Accent
1-1/2 t. ground coriander

Knead all ingredients together. Press together, and make into a long roll. Freeze for three hours, and then cut into slices, putting each patty between waxed paper. Fry as needed.

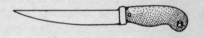

## VEAL CHOPS BRAISED IN CIDER

6 veal loin chops, cut to
 1 inch thickness
salt and pepper to taste
1 t. each dried savory,
 thyme, and paprika
4 T. butter
1 large onion, finely
 chopped
1 cup apple cider, or
 enough to cover chops
2 T. cornstarch combined
 with enough cider to
 dissolve
1-2 apples, sliced and
 dipped in lemon juice, for
 garnish

Preheat oven to 400°F. Sprinkle the chops with the seasonings. Melt 2 tablespoons of the butter in a baking pan that is just large enough to hold the veal chops. Sprinkle the onion over the bottom of the pan. Arrange the chops in one layer in the pan. Melt the remaining butter and pour over the chops. Add the cider. Cover with foil and bake for 45 minutes or until fork tender. Baste occasionally while chops cook. Do not overcook. Transfer the chops to a serving platter and keep warm. Transfer the pan juices to a saucepan and bring to a boil. Thicken with the cornstarch mixture. Adjust seasonings and pour over the chops. Garnish with apples slices if desired. Serve immediately. *Serves 6.*

# SCALOPPINE DI MAIALE *(Pork Scallopini in Wine Sauce)*

In a mortar and pestle or small bowl, combine sage, rosemary, garlic, salt, pepper, and oil to form a smooth paste. Set aside. Remove the rib bone and fat from each chop leaving only the eye. Slice horizontally into two pieces. Place between sheets of waxed paper and pound gently till thin. Press some of the herb mixture into both sides of the pork scallops. Heat the butter and oil, and brown meat on both sides. Remove from pan. Pour off fat. Add wine and return scallops to the pan. Simmer gently 10 to 15 minutes. Remove scallops and place in warm oven. Boil down wine, dissolving bits of cooked meat. Dissolve cornstarch in beef broth and stir in. Cook until thickened. Add parsley and pour over scallopini to serve. *Serves 4.*

2 t. dried sage
2 t. dried rosemary
2 garlic cloves
1/2 t. salt
few grindings fresh pepper
few drops of olive oil
6 center-cut rib pork chops
2 T. butter
2 T. olive oil
3/4 cup dry white wine
1/2 cup beef broth
1 T. cornstarch
2 T. fresh parsley, chopped

# TOURTIÈRE *(Pork Pie)*

**Pastry:** Sift together flour and salt. Cut in shortening and butter. Stir in egg with cold water. Shape dough into a ball. Chill at least 30 minutes; roll out. Makes one double-crust pie.

**Filling:** Combine ingredients and brown in a large skillet. Do not overcook. Drain fat. Make upper and lower crusts for two pies. Fill with meat filling. Bake at 400°F. for 10 minutes, then reduce heat to 350°F. and bake 40 minutes more.

*Pastry:*
2 cups flour
3/4 t. salt
3/4 cup shortening
2 T. butter
1 egg, beaten
3 T. cold water

*Filling:*
1-1/2 lbs. ground pork
1/2 lb. ground beef
2 medium onions, minced
1 T. salt
1/2 t. pepper
1/2 t. cloves
1 clove garlic, minced
1/2 t. cinnamon
3/4 cup water

## APPLEJACK PORK CHOPS WITH GINGER

2 T. butter
2 T. olive or vegetable oil
1 small onion, chopped
1 clove garlic, chopped
8 thin pork chops
salt and pepper to taste
1/2 cup applejack
1 T. chopped parsley
1 T. chopped fresh ginger
   root
1/2 cup veal stock or
   chicken broth

*Apple Garnish:*
butter to sauté the apples
8 1/2-inch thick slices from
   a firm, tart apple, cored
   but not peeled
sugar
2 T. applejack

Put the butter and oil in a skillet, add the onion and garlic, and cook slowly until translucent. Remove from the pan with a slotted spoon and set aside. Sprinkle chops with salt and pepper and sauté them quickly in the remaining butter and oil in the skillet until lightly browned. Heat the applejack in a small saucepan, light it with a match, and pour it over the chops. Sprinkle on the parsley and ginger root, then add the cooked onion and garlic. Add the stock and simmer for 15 to 20 minutes, until the juices in the skillet have formed a sauce. Add a little more stock if necessary. (There should be about a teaspoonful of sauce per chop.) Arrange the chops on a warmed serving platter, cover with the sauce, and keep warm while you prepare the apple garnish.

Add a little butter to the skillet, put in the apple slices, and sprinkle lightly with sugar. Cook over fairly high heat about 2 minutes each side, turning once. Sprinkle with 2 tablespoons applejack, swirl around the pan, and serve the apple slices on the platter with the pork. *Serves 4.*

# CASSEROLES

## BOW TIE CASSEROLE

Brown meat, onion, and half the garlic in oil or butter. Add spinach juice, tomato puree, water, and seasonings. Cook for 15 minutes. In a separate bowl mix chopped spinach, remaining garlic, bread crumbs, half of the grated cheese, salad oil, and eggs. Butter a large casserole and layer half of the ingredients: cooked noodles, spinach and cheese mixture, and meat and tomato mixture. Repeat these layers to fill the casserole and use up the ingredients. Top with remaining cheese. Bake at 350°F. for about an hour, until hot all the way through. This may be refrigerated a day ahead and then baked; it also freezes well. *Serves 8.*

1-1/2 lbs. ground beef
1 large onion, chopped
1 or 2 cloves garlic, minced
oil or butter for browning
1 large (27-ounce) can spinach, drained (or 2-1/2 cups fresh or frozen, cooked), with juice reserved
3/4 cup spinach juice
10 ounces tomato puree
1/2 cup water
1 t. salt
pepper to taste
1 t. mixed herbs (oregano, basil and/or rosemary)
1/4 cup bread crumbs
3/4 cup grated cheese, or more to taste
1/4 cup salad oil
2 eggs, lightly beaten with 1 t. salt
1 12-ounce package bow tie noodles, cooked and drained

## YODELING GOOD SWISS CASSEROLE

1-1/2 lbs. veal cutlets, 1/4
  inch thick
3 T. flour
1 t. salt
1-1/2 cups beef gravy or
  1-3/4 can beef gravy
2 cups of wide noodles,
  cooked
1/2 lb. Swiss cheese, sliced
1-1/2 t. paprika
1/4 cup butter
1/2 cup light cream
2 t. chopped chives

Cut the veal into serving-sized pieces. Place cheese slice on each of half of the veal slices. Top with the second veal piece. Combine the flour, paprika, salt, and use to coat the veal. Brown well in the butter at 325°F., then remove the veal from the skillet. In the same skillet, stir gravy into light cream and simmer for five minutes at 200°F. In a two-quart casserole place alternate layers of noodles, sauce and veal. Sprinkle with the chives. Cover and bake for 1 hour and 30 minutes at 375°F. *Serves 6.*

## RICE TORTE *(from Northern Italy)*

1 cup cooked rice
1/2 lb. hamburger
  (optional)
3 green peppers, chopped
3 onions, chopped
2 eggs, lightly beaten
1 10-ounce package
  spinach, cooked and
  drained
bread crumbs to thicken, if
  needed
oregano, garlic, salt,
  pepper, and thyme to
  taste
1/2 lb. brick cheese, grated
1/2 cup Parmesean cheese,
  grated

Mix all ingredients together and spread in 9" by 13" pan in a layer about 1 inch thick. Bake at 350°F. for 45 minutes. Cut into serving sizes. Tastes good hot or cold.

## HADDOCK CASSEROLE

Poach fish in a large pan until flaky; reserve a little of the water. Melt butter, stir in flour, and gradually stir in mixture of milk and poaching water to make a thick white sauce. Add the cheese to the sauce and heat until the cheese is melted. In a greased casserole, alternate layers of fish and cheese sauce, ending with sauce. Bake uncovered at 350°F. for 30 to 45 minutes.

1 lb. fresh or frozen fish
3 T. butter or margarine
2 to 3 T. flour
1/2 cup milk
1/4 cup poaching liquid
1/2 lb. Cheddar cheese, cut in small chunks or grated
dash of pepper

## CARROT CASSEROLE

Scrape carrots and cut on diagonal, making slices about 1/4 inch thick. Cook in salted water until tender but still crisp. Drain, reserving 1/4 cup cooking liquid. Mix onion, horseradish, mayonnaise, salt, pepper, and carrot liquid; combine with carrots in a buttered casserole. Mix the bread crumbs with the melted butter and spread over the carrots. Bake at 375°F. for 15 to 20 minutes or until bubbly. *Serves 6.*

1 lb. carrots
1/4 cup carrot liquid (see directions)
2 T. grated onion
3/4 t. horseradish
1/2 cup mayonnaise
1/2 t. salt
1/2 t. pepper
1/2 cup seasoned bread crumbs
1/4 cup melted butter

## SHOE PEG CORN CASSEROLE

Combine cheese and butter; mix with corn and chilies. Place in an 8" square pan. (Size and shape are important, so mixture is correct depth.) Bake at 350°F. until bubbly, about 15 minutes.

2 3-ounce packages cream cheese, softened
1-1/2 sticks butter, softened
2 12-ounce cans whole-kernel shoe peg corn (or whole-kernel white)
1 4-ounce can chopped green chilies

## ZUCCHINI AND TOMATO CASSEROLE

2 lbs. fresh zucchini
4 T. butter
2 T. water
1 35-ounce can Italian
    tomatoes (or 1 lb. fresh),
    peeled, seeded, and
    chopped
2 T. fresh basil, chopped
1 garlic clove, pressed
salt and pepper to taste
2 T. Gruyère cheese, grated
2 T. Parmesan cheese,
    grated
1/4 cup buttered bread
    crumbs

Wash and thinly slice zucchini. Melt butter in large skillet. Toss zucchini to coat with melted butter and cook over high heat, stirring continuously. Sprinkle with water and continue to cook until tender, yet firm. Remove from pan, and set aside. Pour tomatoes into skillet. Add basil, garlic, salt, and pepper. Cook until slightly thickened. Pour over zucchini and mix. Spoon into a buttered casserole or individual gratin dishes. Sprinkle with mixture of Gruyère and Parmesan cheese and top with buttered bread crumbs. Cover with foil and bake at 425°F. for 30 minutes. Remove foil and brown crumbs briefly under broiler. *Serves 4.*

## ZUCCHINI-CHEESE CASSEROLE

4 medium zucchini
4 cloves garlic, mashed
1 large onion
5 or 6 eggs
2 lbs. of small-curd cottage
    cheese
1/2 to 1 cup Parmesan
    cheese, grated
1/4 cup fresh parsley,
    chopped
2 10-ounce packages
    frozen chopped spinach,
    cooked and drained (can
    substitute fresh spinach
    or Swiss chard to make 3
    cups cooked vegetable)
1/2 to 1 lb. mozzarella
    cheese, sliced
4 to 5 cups tomato sauce
1/2 to 1 cup bread crumbs

Slice zucchini, brown lightly in 2 tablespoons of butter on both sides, and set aside. Sauté garlic and onion in 2 tablespoons of olive oil. Beat together eggs, cottage cheese, Parmesan cheese, parsley, spinach, garlic, and onions. Add salt and freshly ground pepper to taste. In 9" by 13" pan, layer ingredients like lasagna: a layer of tomato sauce, a layer of fried zucchini, a light sprinkling of bread crumbs seasoned with oregano to taste, a layer of cheese-spinach mixture, a layer of mozzarella. Repeat, ending with a layer of sauce and a sprinkling of Parmesan cheese. Bake 30 minutes covered and 30 minutes uncovered at 350°F. *Serves 12.*

# DAVID REGAMEY'S
# BARLEY AND MUSHROOM CASSEROLE

In a large skillet heat butter and sauté mushrooms 10 minutes, until firm and golden. Remove from pan. Sauté onion until soft. Add barley to skillet and stir till lightly brown. Pour in bouillon, cover pan, and simmer until barley is tender — about 40 minutes or more. Add mushrooms, cottage cheese, sour cream, chives, parsley, salt, and pepper. Mix well. Transfer to baking dish and bake 1 hour at 325°F. Dish can be lightly covered with foil for the last 20 minutes. Sprinkle top with parsley before serving. *Serves 20.*

1/2 cup butter or margarine
1 lb. mushrooms, sliced
1 large sweet onion, chopped
1 lb. barley
5 cups chicken bouillon
1 cup cottage cheese
1 cup sour cream
2 T. chopped chives or scallions
salt and pepper to taste
2 T. minced parsley

# MUSHROOM AND CHEESE CASSEROLE

Butter a casserole dish and then put in layers of mushrooms topped with bread crumbs, onion, and cheese dotted with butter. End with a layer of butter and crumbs topped by the Parmesan cheese. Cover and bake about 30 minutes in a moderate oven (375°F.). To crisp the top, remove the cover for the last five minutes.

1 to 1-1/2 lbs. oyster mushrooms
3 cups soft bread crumbs
2 medium onions, diced
2 cups grated mild Cheddar, Monterey Jack, or other cheese
1/4 cup Parmesan cheese
6 T. butter
salt and pepper to taste

# SOUPS, CHOWDERS & STEWS

### MEDITERRANEAN FISH SOUP

3 T. olive oil
1 large onion, sliced
  (approximately 1 cup)
1 to 2 cloves fresh garlic,
  minced
1/2 cup chopped celery,
  including leaves
1/2 cup coarsely chopped
  green pepper
2 16-ounce cans of
  tomatoes, with their
  juice, or 3 or 4 fresh
  tomatoes, peeled and
  with their juice
1/2 cup white wine
1/2 cup minced parsley
1/8 t. black pepper
salt, to taste
2 threads of saffron
  (optional and expensive,
  but definitely character-
  giving)
1 lb. (approximately) fish
  fillets, from any white,
  semi-firm textured fish:
  cod, haddock, pollock,
  hake, carp, cusk, drum,
  croaker, grouper, or
  rockfish
1 cup cooked rice or
  cooked potato slices
Tabasco sauce, a dash to
  taste

In a large pot, heat the oil and then sauté the onion, garlic, celery, and green pepper. Add the tomatoes and liquid or juice, wine, parsley and spices. Cover and simmer gently for 30 minutes. If mixture looks too thick for soup, thin with stock, tomato juice, or water. Cut the fish into serving-size chunks and gently lay them on the prepared hot broth. Simmer an additional 7 to 10 minutes, until the fish pieces will flake apart easily when probed with a fork. Now add the cooked rice or potatoes, merely to heat through, stirring all ever so gently. Serve the soup in deep bowls, with the Tabasco on the table. Crusty French or Italian breads go well with this, as do hard rolls. The amounts of fish, rice or potatoes, and liquid can be flexible, to accommodate the number of servings desired. These proportions will serve 4 to 6 people depending upon the size of the bowls.

## ITALIAN VEGETABLE SOUP

Sauté mushrooms, garlic, and onions in hot oil. Add seasonings, tomatoes, honey, wine, tamari, and vegetable broth and cook about 1 hour. Add chick peas, zucchini, pepper, and parsley and cook until vegetables are tender. *Serves 6.*

1/4 lb. mushrooms, sliced
3 cloves garlic, minced
2 onions, chopped
2 T. oil
1 t. basil
1 T. oregano
2 bay leaves
pinch of thyme
1/4 t. black pepper
1/4 t. salt
3 cups crushed tomatoes
1 t. honey
1/4 cup white wine
2 T. tamari
2 cups vegetable broth
2 cups chick peas
1 zucchini, sliced fine
1 large pepper, cut in
   julienne strips
2 T. fresh parsley, chopped

## LENTIL SOUP

Cook all ingredients in heavy saucepan till mixture comes to a boil. Let simmer for 30 minutes or longer if desired. Oil in recipe accelerates cooking time.

Cook 1 pound small shells or 1 pound elbows or ditalini macaroni according to package. Strain. Add to lentil soup. Cook for 5 minutes more. *Serves 6.*

1/2 lb. lentils
1-1/2 quarts of water
2 or 3 stalks of celery and
   leaves, chopped fine
2 small carrots, chopped
   fine
chopped parsley (sprinkle)
1 whole onion, chopped
1 clove garlic, chopped
salt and pepper to taste
1 large T. oil
3 fresh ripe tomatoes or 1/2
   cup canned tomatoes
bay leaf

## CHUNKY TOMATO BISQUE

3 T. olive oil
1/2 cup finely diced onion
3/4 cup diced celery
1-1/2 t. freshly crushed
   garlic
3 cups tomato puree
1 cup tomato paste
2-1/2 cups water
1-1/2 t. salt
2 T. parsley
1 T. basil
1/2 t. white pepper
2 t. paprika
1/2 t. cinnamon
1/4 t. cayenne
3 medium tomatoes, diced
1 T. honey
1 T. wine vinegar
4 cups milk
freshly grated Parmesan
   cheese

An unusually flavored thick soup. The cinnamon flavor becomes more pronounced if the soup sits for a few days.

In a heavy pan sauté the onion in the oil for 3 minutes. Add the celery and garlic and sauté 3 minutes more, stirring often. Add the puree, paste, water, and spices. Bring the mixture slowly to a boil and then simmer for at least 15 minutes. Add the diced tomatoes and simmer for 10 minutes more. Stir in the honey and vinegar, then gradually stir in the milk. Bring the soup to just below a boil and serve immediately. Garnish with the Parmesan. *Serves 8 generously.*

## SUNNY ACRES CORN CHOWDER

4 medium potatoes, cubed
4 medium onions, sliced
6 T. butter
4 cups milk
1/2 cup light cream
2 large cans creamed corn
1-1/2 t. salt
1/8 t. pepper
1/4 t. parsley, or more to
   taste
1/8 t. thyme
1/8 t. marjoram

Cook cubed potatoes in water to cover for 15 minutes. Meanwhile, fry onions in 2 tablespoons of the butter. Warm the milk and cream in a large kettle and add potatoes (drain the potatoes and save 1/2 cup of the liquid to rinse out the corn cans, then add to soup), onions, corn, remaining 4 tablespoons butter, salt, pepper, and herbs. Heat mixture to piping hot, but don't boil. For better flavor, set aside to cool and then reheat. *Serves 6 to 8.*

## MILDRED'S CHOWDER

Dice salt pork and bacon and brown slowly until fat is rendered. Meanwhile, cook haddock fillets in water to cover; when cooked, lift out with a slotted spatula and set aside. Peel and dice potatoes and cook in the fish cooking water. Peel and chop onions and add to the cooked bacon and salt pork. Cook slowly until onions are transparent. Combine fish, cooked potatoes and cooking water, onions, salt pork, and bacon in a heavy soup pot. Add minced clams, small shrimp, niblet corn, and mix well. Stir in heavy cream and add enough milk to give chowder desired consistency. Add salt and pepper to taste.

1 2-inch piece of salt pork
2 slices bacon
1 lb. haddock fillets
4 or 5 potatoes
4 medium onions
2 cans minced clams
1 can small shrimp
1 can niblet corn
1/2 pint heavy cream
1 quart milk (or enough to achieve desired consistency)
salt and pepper to taste

## SEAFOOD CHOWDER

Dice potatoes and cook in stock made from fish bones. Sauté onions in butter until soft and add to potatoes. Add raw seafood and cook. When potatoes are done, fish will be done, too. Season with salt and pepper. Add one can of cream-style corn. Using half heavy cream and half light cream, add cream to chowder and bring to a scald. Do not boil. Do not thicken.

2 potatoes
1 onion
1/2 lb. haddock or skinless cod fillets
1/4 lb. scallops
6 oysters with liquor
1/4 lb. shrimp, peeled and deveined
3 large chowder clams, minced raw (remove stomachs — they will darken the chowder too much)
1 can cream-style corn
1 pt. light cream
1 pt. heavy cream

### OVEN FISH CHOWDER

2 T. olive oil
2 lbs. boneless and skinless fish of any kind, fresh or thawed, cut into slices
1/2 t. dried thyme
1 lemon, peeled, pitted, and sliced very thin
1 medium onion, peeled and sliced thin
2 garlic cloves, peeled and sliced thin
2 stalks celery (including leaves), diced
3 large tomatoes, peeled and sliced
3 medium potatoes, peeled and cut in half lengthwise
1/2 cup coarsely chopped fresh parsley
2 T. olive oil
3/4 cup white wine
1 t. salt, or more to taste
pepper
6 cups water
1 T. Worcestershire sauce

Use a 4-quart ovenproof pot with a tight-fitting lid. Cover the bottom of the pot with 2 tablespoons olive oil. Arrange fish over the oil. Dust with thyme. Arrange in layers over the fish, the lemon, onion, garlic, celery, tomatoes, potatoes, and parsley. Dribble 2 tablespoons olive oil over this and pour in white wine. Add salt and pepper. Add water and Worcestershire sauce. Put the lid on the pot and place in a preheated 375°F. oven for 1 hour. Remove the potato halves with a slotted spoon and purée them in the blender with a cup or more of the soup liquid. Put the purée back in the pot, break up the pieces of fish with a spoon, and stir well before serving. *Serves 6 to 8.*

### LAMB STEW WITH YOGURT

1 T. butter
1-1/2 lbs. lamb stew meat
1 t. salt
3/4 t. dill weed
2 cups water
4 or 5 medium potatoes, peeled and quartered
4 or 5 carrots, peeled and cut in 2-inch pieces
3 or 4 stalks celery, cut in 2-inch pieces
1 cup plain yogurt
2 T. flour

Melt butter in heavy pot and brown meat on all sides. Add salt, dill weed, and water. Cover and simmer for about 1 hour, until meat is almost tender. Add potatoes, carrots, and celery and simmer for 30 additional minutes, until vegetables are tender. In a small bowl, combine yogurt and flour with a whisk. Remove meat and vegetables to warmed serving dish and add yogurt mixture to liquid in pan. Cook over low heat, stirring constantly, until thickened; then cook 2 minutes longer. Pour gravy over lamb and vegetables. *Serves 4.*

# POULTRY

## THE SULTAN'S FAVORITE

Simmer chicken with celery and onion in lightly salted water until tender. Remove meat from bones in large pieces. Strain and reserve stock. Melt butter in saucepan, blend in flour, and gradually add milk and stock. Cook over low heat until thick and smooth, stirring constantly. Remove from heat and add curry powder, lemon juice, and mayonnaise. Beat with rotary beater until very smooth. Cook and drain broccoli. Arrange in bottom of greased 3-quart casserole. Place pieces of chicken on top and pour sauce over all. Garnish with pimiento strips and bake at 400°F. for 20 minutes or until heated through. *Serves 8.*

2 broiler/fryers, or a 5-lb. fowl
2 stalks celery
1 medium onion
salt
2-1/2 cups water
6 T. butter
1/2 cup flour
1 cup milk
2 cups strained chicken stock
1 t. curry powder
1 t. lemon juice
1 cup mayonaise
2 10-ounce packages frozen broccoli
pimiento strips

## CHICKEN CACCIATORE

Fry chicken in heavy skillet in oil. When all pieces are golden brown, add onion, garlic, salt, pepper, and red pepper flakes. Sauté until slightly browned. Add tomato paste and mix well. Add tomatoes and turn till all pieces are well coated. Add juice only from can of peas. Lightly salt and pepper again. Sauté for 25 minutes.

Add peppers and mushrooms and sauté for 10 minutes. Add can of peas. *Do not mix or cook anymore.* Turn off stove and let sit for 5 minutes. Sprinkle with fresh chopped parsley. *Serves 5.*

1 chicken, cut in small pieces
oil to cover bottom of pan
1 large onion, chopped
1 large clove garlic, chopped
salt and pepper to taste
pinch of red pepper flakes
1 T. tomato paste
1 medium can crushed tomatoes
1 large can peas
2 or 3 green peppers, sliced thick
1/2 to 3/4 lb. mushrooms (if small, don't cut; if large, cut in large chunks)
parsley to taste

## SKILLET CHICKEN TETRAZZINI

1 3-lb. chicken
2-1/2 cups water
1/4 t. pepper
salt
8 ounces noodles
margarine or butter
1 small onion, minced
1/4 cup flour
1/4 t. rosemary
paprika
1/2 cup half-and-half-cream
1 T. Parmesan cheese

Place chicken breast-side down in large pot. Add water, pepper, and 2 teaspoons salt. Over high heat bring to boil. Reduce heat to low, cover pot, and simmer 35 minutes. Remove chicken to large bowl, refrigerate 30 minutes. Meanwhile strain broth, reserving 2 cups. When chicken is cool, cut meat into bite-size pieces, discarding bones and skin. Set chicken aside. Prepare noodles as directed on box; drain. In large skillet over medium heat, melt 2 tablespoons butter or margarine, add onion, and cook until tender. Remove onion and melt 3 tablespoons more butter, stir in flour, rosemary, 1 teaspoon salt, and 1/4 teaspoon paprika. Gradually add chicken broth and cook, stirring constantly, until thick. Stir in cream, chicken, noodles, and onion, and cook over low heat until mixture is heated through. Sprinkle with Parmesan cheese and paprika. *Serves 6.*

## CURRIED CHICKEN

2-3 t. curry powder
1/2 t. mint flakes, crushed
1/2 t. sage leaves, crushed
1/4 t. salt
2 t. lemon juice
1 broiler chicken, cut up
3 T. oil
1 cup water (or less)
1 t. sesame seeds

Make a paste of the curry, mint, sage, salt, and lemon juice, and spread it over the chicken pieces. Heat the oil in a heavy pan and brown the chicken for about 10 minutes. Add water, cover, and simmer for 20 minutes. Turn pieces and continue cooking about 25 minutes longer, until tender. Sprinkle with sesame seeds before serving. *Serves 4.*

# CHICKEN JEREZ

Rub chickens generously with softened butter; dust lightly with salt. Combine all ingredients for the stuffing, chopping the livers and almonds. Fill cavities of the chickens loosely with rice mixture. Arrange chickens in a large shallow flower pot — the dish type. Baste with sherry as they roast in preheated 350°F. oven for 45 minutes, or until drumsticks move easily.

As the chickens roast, make stock by cooking necks and giblets in salted water; boil stock down to one cup. Combine chicken stock with liquid in casserole after chickens are removed, thickening sauce lightly if preferred. Taste for salt. Serve sauce with roasted stuffed chickens, allowing half a chicken per person.

Jerez is the region in Spain where chicken is cooked like this. Also where a great deal of sherry is made.

2 broilers (2 lbs. each) left whole
softened butter
1/4 cup sherry (a must)

*Stuffing:*
3 cups cooked rice
1/4 cup chopped ham
6 almonds blanched and sautéed
2 chicken livers sautéed
1 T. minced parsley
2 T. melted butter

# ROAST DUCKLING

Rub duck inside and out with 1 teaspoon of curry, garlic, Tabasco, and turmeric. Stuff with rice stuffing. Roast at 325°F. for 3 hours. Baste during the baking with honey, lemon juice, orange juice and a teaspoon of curry, mixed. Prick skin all over often during baking. Serve duck quartered. Garnish with kumquats and parsley.

**Rice Stuffing:** Melt butter, sauté onion and celery. Add rest of ingredients, and stuff duck. Serve with duck quarters. (Plain rice may be flavored by adding chicken bouillon cube or instant bouillon to water in which rice is cooked.)

1 Long Island duckling
2 t. curry powder, divided
1 clove garlic, chopped
1/4 t. Tabasco
1 t. turmeric
1/4 cup honey
1/4 cup each lemon and orange juice

*Rice Stuffing:*
2 T. butter
3 T. chopped onion
3 T. chopped celery
2 cups bread cubes
1 t. salt
pepper to taste
2 cans mandarin oranges or 4 oranges peeled and sectioned
1 t. poultry seasoning
1-1/2 cups cooked rice

# ROCK CORNISH GAME HENS
# WITH ORANGE GLAZE

2 Cornish game hens

*Bread Stuffing:*
1/3 cup butter
2 or 3 cloves garlic, minced
2 small onions, chopped
2 stalks celery, sliced
6 mushrooms, sliced
1/4 cup raisins
1/4 cup freshly chopped
   parsley
1 t. tarragon
1 t. dill
1/2 t. sage
1/2 cup chicken broth
1 cup fresh bread crumbs
4 to 6 fresh oysters

*Orange Glaze:*
8 ounces orange
   marmalade
1 T. Grand Marnier
1 T. fresh orange juice
2 large oranges, sliced

Prepare cavities of hens for stuffing by washing out with cold water. Sprinkle cavities with salt.

**Bread Stuffing:** Melt butter in frying pan and sauté garlic, onion, and celery until soft. Add mushrooms and all remaining ingredients except broth, bread crumbs, and oysters. When well blended add broth; then add bread crumbs and stir until liquid is taken up. (Add more crumbs if mixture is too moist.) Stuff hens, inserting 2 or 3 oysters in each hen with the stuffing. Place in baking pan and lightly butter the skins. Bake in a preheated 350°F. oven for 30 minutes before adding orange glaze.

**Orange Glaze:** In a small pan, heat marmalade, liqueur, and juice and cook slightly. Pour glaze over hens and continue to cook until done (about 1 hour and 30 minutes total cooking time), basting occasionally. Garnish with fresh orange slices and serve immediately.

# BAKED CORNISH HENS WITH HONEY SAUCE

6 Cornish game hens
salt and pepper
1/2 cup honey
1/2 cup white-wine
   Worcestershire sauce
   (lighter in color and
   taste than regular
   Worcestershire sauce)

Wash hens and remove giblets to use for gravy or stuffing. Season hens inside and out with salt and pepper. Place in roasting pan and bake at 350°F. for 1 hour and 15 minutes. Mix honey and white-wine Worcestershire sauce together and after the first 30 minutes of cooking baste hens every 10 minutes with the mixture. *Serves 6.*

# BOURBON PECAN TURKEY

rumble cornbread, set aside. Sauté onion, elery, pecans, and ham in butter or margarine bout 3 minutes). Add mixture to cornbread ong with parsley, chervil, thyme, bourbon, g, and turkey stock. Season with salt and epper.

ornbread: Preheat oven to 400°F. Combine ry ingredients in bowl; set aside. In a small owl, stir honey into softened butter or marrine; add egg and buttermilk. Add this mixre to dry ingredients, stirring until just ixed. Pour into well-buttered 8" by 8" square an and bake in 400°F. oven about 25 minutes. ool and crumble for dressing. For drier ressing, spread crumbs on a cookie sheet in low (200°F.) oven until dry.

ourbon Pecan Basting Sauce: Melt butter ver low heat. Put pecans and bourbon in lender; blend. Combine bourbon-pecan mixre, butter, and honey. Do not boil.

lace turkey breast-side down and season cavy with half the basting sauce. Stuff and preare turkey for roasting. Baste every half hour nd when turkey is roasted, set on a large platr and make the gravy.

ourbon Pecan Gravy: Add remaining bastg sauce to pan and stir in 1/2 cup of flour, ooking about 5 minutes and mixing in all the rowned bits from the sides of pan. If there a lot of grease in the pan drippings, skim it ff, leaving about 1/2 cup to mix with the lour. Add turkey stock and cook, stirring until ravy is thickened and smooth. Season with alt, pepper, and bourbon. For meat gravy, add hopped meat and pecans.

lace turkey on a large platter and trim with prigs of parsley and lemons cut in half and illed with a meat relish. Or just decorate with vhole unshelled pecans.

10-12 lb. turkey
*Bourbon Pecan Dressing:*
1 cornbread recipe (see below)
1/2 medium onion, diced
1 cup celery, diced
1 cup pecans, diced
1 cup ham, diced
1/2 cup butter or margarine
1/2 cup fresh parsley, chopped
1 T. chervil (optional)
2 t. thyme
1/4 cup bourbon
1 egg, beaten
1/2 cup turkey stock
1 t. salt
1/2 t. black pepper
*Cornbread:*
1 cup cornmeal (white or yellow)
1 cup flour
1 t. baking soda
1 t. baking powder
1/2 t. salt
2 T. honey
1/3 cup butter or margarine, softened
1 egg
1 cup buttermilk
*Bourbon Pecan Basting Sauce:*
1/2 cup butter or margarine
1/4 cup finely diced pecans
1/2 cup bourbon
2 t. honey
*Bourbon Pecan Gravy:*
any remaining basting sauce
1/2 cup flour
drippings from roasting pan
4 cups turkey stock
salt and pepper to taste
1 T. bourbon (or to taste)
turkey giblets, cooked and chopped
1/2 cup pecans, chopped (optional)

# NOBLE ROMAN BIRD

10-12 lb. turkey

*Noble Roman Dressing:*
1 loaf Italian bread, 8 ounces, cubed
1 cup Parmesan cheese, grated
1/2 cup fresh parsley, chopped
1/2 cup margarine or olive oil, or 1/4 cup each
2 cups ham, diced
3 cloves garlic, crushed
1 cup carrots, diced
1 cup celery, diced
2 cups mushrooms, sliced
2 medium tomatoes, fresh, skinned, chopped (or 2 whole canned tomatoes, drained, chopped)
1 t. basil
1 t. oregano
1 cup turkey stock
1/2 cup white wine
salt and pepper to taste

*Noble Roman Basting Sauce:*
2 garlic cloves, crushed
1/2 cup ham, minced or ground
1/2 cup margarine or olive oil (or 1/4 cup each)
2 cups tomato sauce
1 t. basil
1 t. oregano
3-4 peppercorns
2 t. chervil
1 bay leaf
1/2 t. fennel seed
1/2 t. salt

**Noble Roman Dressing:** Toss bread, Parmesan cheese, and parsley together in a large mixing bowl; set aside. In a large frying pan, melt margarine and/or olive oil and sauté ham, garlic, carrots, celery, and mushrooms about 5 minutes or until just limp. Add tomatoes, basil and oregano, cooking 2 more minutes. Stir in turkey stock and white wine. Pour this mixture over bread, cheese, and parsley and mix together, adding more stock or wine, if desired. Salt and pepper to taste.

**Noble Roman Basting Sauce:** Sauté garlic and ham in margarine or olive oil for about 2 minutes and then add all other ingredients; simmer sauce 15 to 20 minutes. Reserve 1 cup of this sauce for basting.

With turkey breast-side down, season cavity with the Noble Roman basting sauce and stuff with Noble Roman Dressing. Roast, basting every half hour. When turkey is roasted, place on platter and make Noble Roman Gravy.

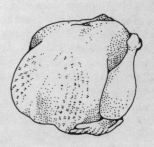

## NOBLE ROMAN BIRD *(continued)*

**Noble Roman Gravy:** When turkey is arranged on platter, pour liquid from roasting pan into a bowl and let fat rise to surface. Return 6 tablespoons of fat to roasting pan, stir in 6 tablespoons of flour, and cook about 2 minutes, stirring constantly. Stir in turkey stock, remaining basting sauce, white wine, and liquid from roasting pan (degreased). Cook, stirring until gravy is thickened and smooth. Add salt and pepper to taste. Arrange turkey on a large platter lined with fresh spinach leaves, and decorate with fresh mushrooms and olives.

*Noble Roman Gravy:*
pan drippings
6 T. flour
3 cups turkey stock
any remaining basting sauce
1/2 cup white wine
salt and pepper to taste

# SEAFOOD

## ROLLED STUFFED FISH FILLETS

4 skinless, boneless fillets
of sole or flounder (each
approximately 8" by 4"
or 5")
1 cup soft bread crumbs
1/2 cup wheat cracker
crumbs
2 T. chopped parsley
6 T. melted butter
2 T. dry sherry

Preheat oven to 400°F. Place fillets, skinned side up, on a flat surface. Combine the bread and cracker crumbs with parsley, 3 tablespoons melted butter, and 1 tablespoon sherry. Toss gently. Center equal portions of the filling on top of the fillets and spread evenly, leaving a slight margin on all sides. Roll up each fillet and secure with a long toothpick or skewer. Put remaining 3 tablespoons of butter and 1 tablespoon of sherry in shallow baking dish and place in oven for several minutes until hot. Place fish rolls in the baking dish; baste with butter-sherry sauce. Bake for 15 minutes, turning once with tongs. If difficult to manipulate, skip the turning (it's not absolutely necessary). *Serves 4.*

## GOOD FRIDAY SOLE *(Fish Roll-Ups)*

4 lbs. small fillets of sole
(or 5 large fillets)
seasoned bread crumbs
1 can Campbell's shrimp
soup
1/2 can milk
1 package Knorr's leek
soup mix
4-1/2 cups milk
1/3 cup sherry (optional)
1 lb. raw shrimp, peeled
and deveined
fresh parsley, chopped

Sprinkle fish fillets with bread crumbs, roll up, and fasten with toothpicks. Place rolls in a flat baking dish. In a large pan, combine shrimp soup, 1/2 can of milk, leek soup mix, and 4-1/2 cups of milk. Bring to a boil and simmer for 10 minutes. Add sherry and heat. Add raw shrimp. Pour mixture over fish fillets and bake at 250°F. for about 25 minutes, until fish tests done. Garnish rolls with fresh parsley and serve. *Serves 8-10.*

## SHAD BAKED IN CREAM

Preheat oven to 400°F. Butter a baking dish and place shad in it. Dot with butter and sprinkle with salt and pepper. Bake uncovered for 20 minutes. Add the cream and bake 10 minutes longer, basting with the cream. Sprinkle with the parsley. *Serves 6.*

· 1 3-lb. boned shad
butter
salt and freshly ground
   pepper to taste
1 cup heavy cream
chopped parsley

## BAKED FISH FIESTA

Thaw frozen fish, cut into 6 equal portions. Combine crumbs, 2 tablespoons cheese, parsley, salt, pepper, and garlic. Dip fish in oil, drain and dip in crumb mixture. Place fillets in individual baking pans or on baking sheet. Fry bacon pieces until half done; drain well. Top each fish portion with an equal amount of bacon, tomato pieces and egg slices. Sprinkle with remaining 2 tablespoons of cheese. Bake in moderate oven at 375°F. for 20 minutes or until fish flakes easily when tested with a fork.

2 lbs. cusk, cod or other
   firm fish fillets, fresh or
   frozen
3/4 cup fine dry bread
   crumbs
1/4 cup grated Parmesan
   cheese
2 T. chopped parsley
1 t. salt
1/4 t. pepper
1 small clove garlic,
   minced
1/4 cup cooking oil
3 slices bacon, diced
1 can (8 ounces) stewed
   tomatoes (or 1 cup
   chopped tomatoes)
2 hard-cooked eggs, sliced

## BROILED BLUEFISH WITH ROSEMARY, SOY, AND GARLIC

2 lbs. bluefish fillets
4 large garlic cloves
2 T. soy sauce
1 t. fresh rosemary leaves
(no stalks) or 1/2 t. dried

Preheat the broiler, with the rack about 4 inches from the heat source. Oil a broiler pan and place fish on pan, skin side down. Push garlic through a garlic press and spread evenly over fish with a table knife. Sprinkle fish with soy sauce, then with rosemary leaves. Broil until rosemary is slightly toasted but not burned and center of fish is just firm when pressed gently, 10 to 12 minutes (timing varies depending on thickness of fish). Cut into serving portions and serve immediately. *Serves 4.*

## MARINATED FISH WITH SOUR CREAM

1 lb. fish fillets
1/2 cup oil
1/4 cup lemon juice
1 clove garlic
1 T. minced onion
3 T. parsley, chopped
1 T. lemon rind, grated
1/2 t. rosemary
1/2 t. salt
1/2 t. pepper
1/2 cup flour
1 T. Parmesan cheese,
grated
1/2 t. paprika
1/2 cup sour cream

Marinate fish fillets for several hours at room temperature in mixture of oil, lemon juice, garlic, onion, parsley, lemon rind, rosemary, salt, and pepper. Dredge fish in flour mixed with salt, pepper, Parmesan cheese, and paprika. Fry fish in hot oil until brown, then lay in baking pan and spread with sour cream. Bake at 350°F. until fish is done. *Serves 3.*

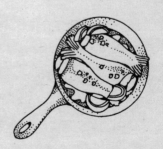

## DEVILED CRAB

Toss crabmeat gently with lemon juice. Sprinkle in mustard, white pepper, Worcestershire sauce, and Tabasco, Melt butter. Toss seasoned crab very lightly in the butter — do not break up the chunks of crabmeat. Add cream if desired. Grease 4 large scallop shells or individual baking dishes with margarine. Mound one-quarter of the crabmeat lightly into each shell. Mask with a thin coating of mayonnaise. Sprinkle with seasoned bread crumbs. Bake at 250°F. until heated through and so crumbs are a little crunchy. *Serves 4.*

2 6-ounce packages fresh
  crabmeat
juice of 1/2 lemon
1/4 t. Coleman's dry
  English mustard
1/8 t. white pepper
4 t. Worcestershire sauce
1/2 t. Tabasco sauce
4 T. (1/2 stick) butter
1/4 cup heavy cream
  (optional)
1/2 cup mayonnaise
seasoned bread crumbs

## SCALLOPED OYSTERS CORMIER

Slice bread 1-inch thick and cut it into 1-inch cubes. Grind crackers, melt butter, and mix together. In a large bowl, mix bread and 2/3 of the cracker-butter mixture. Add cream, salt, pepper, and parsley flakes. Slowly add milk and allow mixture to absorb it; mixture should be the consistency of a bread pudding. Add oysters to mixture. Pour into a buttered 2-quart casserole or soufflé dish. Top with remaining cracker-butter mix. Bake at 350°F. for 1 hour and 15 minutes. *Serves 6-8.*

1 loaf French bread
1/2 lb. Ritz crackers
1/2 lb. butter
1 pint all-purpose or light
  cream
1 t. salt
1/2 t. black pepper
1 cup dehydrated parsley
  flakes
approximately 1 quart milk
1 pint oysters

## SAM FINE'S CLAM CAKES

Combine all ingredients to make a stiff batter. Drop by spoonfuls in boiling oil and deep-fry until browned. *Makes about 60.*

12 cups flour
6 eggs
2 T. baking powder
1/2 cup molasses
1 quart milk
10 lbs. chopped clams
seasonings to taste
cooking oil for deep-frying

## FRESH SHRIMP AND SPINACH PIE

3 packages fresh spinach
2 T. butter
2 cans cream of celery
  soup
1-1/2 cups milk
1/4 package of Knorr's leek
  soup mix
1/4 t. white pepper
2 T. curry powder
1/2 t. thyme leaves
1 cup sharp Cheddar
  cheese, shredded
1-1/2 lbs. fresh raw shrimp,
  peeled and deveined
paprika

Wash spinach; drain. Place half of it in a large pot and pour 1 cup of boiling water over it. Cover and let stand for 5 minutes to wilt spinach. Add second half of spinach, mix gently and heat briefly to bring water to a boil. Cover and let stand. Drain. Add butter. Cut up and set aside. Heat celery soup with milk and leek soup mix, plus pepper, curry powder, thyme, and cheese. Cook for 10 minutes over low heat, stirring carefully. Remove from heat and cover until ready to use. Line the bottom of a 9" by 13" baking dish with the cooked spinach. Place shrimp on top of the spinach and pour sauce over shrimp. Dust with paprika. Bake in 250°F. oven until mixture bubbles. Do not overcook. *Serves 12.*

## SCAMPI

2 lbs. medium-sized shrimp
1/2 cup butter
1/2 cup olive oil
1/4 cup onion, minced
1 T. garlic, minced
2 T. lemon juice
4 T. fresh parsley, chopped
1/2 cup dry white wine
salt and pepper to taste

Remove shrimp from the shell and devein. Rinse under cold water and drain on paper toweling. Pat dry. In a large skillet, heat butter and oil. Sauté onion and garlic until translucent. Add wine, lemon juice, parsley, salt, and pepper. Drop in shrimp and cook about 5 minutes or until firm. Transfer to ovenproof platter. Broil briefly until tops are browned. *Serves 6.*

# BOW'S LOBSTER PIE

Plunge lobsters into 4 cups of boiling salted water and boil for exactly 16 minutes. Remove from water and let cool. Pick out meat and place in large shallow casserole or 9" by 12" baking dish. Be sure to include the tomalley (liver). Pour sherry over lobster meat. Melt butter in the top of a double boiler and add flour to make a roux. Blend well with a whisk. Add salt, pepper, and lemon juice; add cream gradually, whisking the mixture to ensure smoothness. Stir until mixture thickens. Add some of the sauce to the beaten egg yolks and whisk together; add the egg mixture to the remaining white sauce. Keep over low heat until mixture is the consistency of soft custard. Cool and pour over lobster meat. Cover with topping of bread crumbs and crushed potato chips (use blender to crush chips). Sprinkle with paprika. Bake in a slow (275°F.) oven until heated through. Decorate if desired with the lobster head and claws. *Serves 8.*

4 1-1/4 lb. lobsters
1/2 cup dry sherry
1 stick butter (1/4 lb.)
5 T. flour
1/2 t. Lawry's seasoned salt
1/8 t. white pepper
2 T. lemon juice
1 cup light cream
4 egg yolks, well beaten
1/4 cup seasoned bread crumbs
1 cup potato chips
paprika

# DEEP-DISH QUAHOG PIE

Melt 2 tablespoons of the butter. Add clams, clam juice, onion, crumbs, egg, milk, parsley, salt and pepper and simmer together for 10 to 12 minutes. Put the mixture in an unlined deep-dish pie pan. Dot with bits of remaining 1 tablespoon butter. Cover with pie crust. Bake at 425°F. for 10 minutes; then reduce heat to 350°F. and bake 30 minutes more, or until lightly browned.

3 T. butter
2 to 2-1/4 cups finely chopped clams (or 4 6-1/2-ounce cans)
1/4 cup clam juice
1 small onion, chopped
1/4 cup cracker crumbs
1 large egg, beaten
1 cup milk
1 sprig minced parsley
sea salt and pepper to taste
1 9-inch unbaked pie shell

# VEGETABLES

## SPINACH LASAGNA

1 lb. ricotta cheese
2 cups shredded
  mozzarella cheese
  (divided)
1 egg
1 package frozen chopped
  spinach, thawed
1 t. salt
1 t. oregano
dash pepper
4 cups (32 ounces)
  spaghetti sauce
9 lasagna noodles,
  uncooked (or enough to
  fit pan)
1 cup water

In a large bowl, mix ricotta cheese, 1 cup of mozzarella cheese, egg, spinach, salt, oregano, and pepper. In a greased 9" by 13" pan layer 1 cup sauce, 3 of the noodles, and half of the cheese mixture. Repeat. Top with remaining noodles and sauce. Sprinkle with remaining 1 cup mozzarella. Pour water around the edges of the pan. Cover tightly with foil and bake at 350°F. for 1 hour and 15 minutes. Let stand for 15 minutes before serving. Can be assembled ahead of time and refrigerated until ready to bake. *Serves 6.*

## SPINACH BARS

4 T. butter
3 eggs
1 cup flour
1 cup milk
1 t. salt
1 t. baking powder
1 lb. Cheddar cheese,
  grated
1 10-ounce package frozen
  chopped spinach, thawed
  and drained
1 small onion, chopped
1/2 cup chopped
  mushrooms (optional)

In a 9" by 13" pan, melt the butter. Mix remaining ingredients together and spoon into pan. Bake at 350°F. for 35 minutes. Cool slightly before cutting into squares. Can be served hot or at room temperature.

**Note:** Frozen chopped broccoli (10-ounce package, thawed) may be substituted for the spinach.

## BROCCOLI WITH SHALLOTS

Cut the broccoli tops off the stems and separate into florets. Peel the stems, cut in quarters lengthwise, and cut the quarters in half crosswise. Peel and chop the shallot in 1/8-inch dice. Squeeze the shallot in a clean dish towel to remove bitter juices. Cream the butter in a small bowl with a fork. Add the squeezed shallot, parsley, salt, and pepper to taste. Set aside to let flavors blend. Steam the broccoli and place in a bowl. Taste the shallot butter for seasoning and add to the broccoli. Toss just to melt the butter, and serve.

1 head broccoli
1 large shallot
3 T. butter
1 T. freshly chopped parsley
1/4 t. salt, approximately freshly ground black pepper

## BROCCOLI PUFF

Cook broccoli about 5 minutes. Drain. Put in 9" by 13" baking dish. Stir together soup, cheese, milk, mayonnaise, and egg. Pour over broccoli. Combine crumbs and butter. Sprinkle over top. Bake at 350°F. for 45 minutes, until browned and bubbling.

1 lb. fresh broccoli
1 can cream of mushroom soup
2 ounces (1/2 cup) shredded Cheddar cheese
1/4 cup milk
1/4 cup mayonnaise
1 egg, beaten
1/4 cup dry bread crumbs
1 T. melted butter

## BRUSSELS SPROUTS WITH SUN-DRIED TOMATO

Rinse the brussels sprouts and cook them in boiling water until crisp-tender. Pour into colander to drain, then submerge in ice water to cool. Drain, then transfer to a bowl. Add tomatoes and toss to combine. In a large glass measuring cup, combine rice wine vinegar, olive oil, garlic, sugar, and Tabasco. Whisk to blend. Pour over brussels sprouts and tomatoes. Add scallions and parsley. Stir gently, then refrigerate. Serve chilled. *Serves 20.*

3 lbs. fresh brussels sprouts
1/2 cup oil-packed, sun-dried tomatoes, cut into thin strips
1/2 cup rice wine vinegar
1/2 cup olive oil
2 cloves garlic, minced
1 T. sugar
dash of Tabasco sauce
4 scallions, thinly sliced
1/2 cup chopped fresh parsley

## MUSHROOMS A LA GRECQUE

2 lbs. small mushrooms
1/2 cup olive oil
1 T. minced garlic
1/2 cup red wine vinegar
1 T. coriander seeds
1 bay leaf
1/2 t. thyme
1/2 t. pepper

Cut any large mushrooms in half. Heat oil in a large pan and add garlic. Do not brown. When oil is quite hot add vinegar, coriander, bay leaf, thyme, and pepper. Cover and cook, shaking pan, for 1 minute. Add mushrooms and cover. Cook over high heat for 7 minutes, uncovering often to stir mushrooms. Remove from heat. Transfer mixture to a glass jar. (There will be about 1-1/2 pints.) Let cool to room temperature and refrigerate for several days. Can also be served right after chilling.

## ZUCCHINI PIE

2 unbaked pie shells
2 lbs. zucchini
1/4 lb. mushrooms
1 large onion
2 cloves garlic
2 T. butter
2 T. sherry
1/2 t. basil
1/2 t. thyme
1/2 t. oregano
1/2 t. ginger
salt and pepper to taste
4 eggs
2-1/2 cups grated cheese —
use a combination of
mozzarella, Swiss, and
Cheddar

Chop vegetables and sauté in butter until limp but not overcooked. Add sherry and seasonings. Add beaten eggs and cheese. Pour into pie shells and bake at 350°F. for 45 to 50 minutes, until lightly browned.

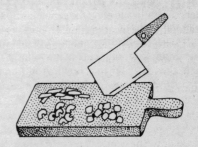

## STUFFED ARTICHOKES

Soak 6 medium artichokes in cold water for about 30 minutes to release dirt. Stand on counter and trim points off leaves with scissors; cut off bottoms so they will be flat to sit in the pan. Stand artichokes upside down and give them a firm whack so that the leaves will open slightly to put in stuffing.

Mix enough oil with bread to moisten. Add remaining ingredients, mix well, and fill insides of the leaves.

Place stuffed artichokes in pan of water (1-1/4 cups) to which 1 teaspoon of salt and 3 cloves or crushed garlic have been added. Sprinkle more oil on top of artichokes and simmer slowly for about 45 minutes.

1-1/2 cups soft Italian bread, grated
1/4 cup freshly chopped parsley
1/2 cup grated cheese (Romano)
salt and pepper to taste
1 clove garlic, finely chopped
oil

## STUFFED ONIONS

Soak the stale rolls in warm milk and squeeze out. Combine the rolls with meats, eggs, and seasonings, and mix well. Peel onions, leaving them whole, and simmer for 20 minutes. Scoop out the centers carefully and chop the center portion before adding to the meat stuffing. Grease a baking pan with the butter. Stuff the onions and place them in the pan. Sprinkle with crumbs and cheese, and pour stock over the top. Bake for 30 minutes in a 350°F. oven. *Serves 4*.

2 stale rolls
1/2 cup milk, warmed
2 ounces cooked ham, chopped
2 ounces leftover meat, minced
2 eggs
chopped parsley, salt, pepper, marjoram to taste
8 onions
2 T. butter
4 T. grated cheese
1 T. bread crumbs
1 cup beef stock

## COURGETTES VERTES ET JAUNES AUX HERBES DE PROVENCE
### (Zucchini with Yellow Squash with Provençal Herbs)

2 yellow summer squash
(3 if smaller)
2 zucchini (3 if smaller)
1-1/2 T. clarified butter or
other fat or oil of your
choice
salt
pepper from the mill
Provençal herbs, fresh or
dried (available in jars)

There are two ways of cutting the vegetables for this presentation. If both varieties of squash are small and without visible seeds, slice them into 1/6-inch slices, then recut the slices lengthwise into 1/6-inch strips. Should the squash be older and larger, "box" each of them, that is, remove the skin of each in four longitudinal bands, leaving 1/8 inch of flesh attached to the skin. The center is good for a soup. Cut each long band on the slant into 1/6-inch-wide julienne strips.

Prepare the julienne of vegetables as indicated above. Stir-fry in clarified butter or oil and add the herbs. If the herbs are dried, powder them well before adding to the pan. Mix well. *Serves 6.*

## CARROT-POTATO PANCAKES

3 medium-size baking
potatoes, peeled
3 eggs, lightly beaten
1/4 cup milk
1/3 cup flour, unsifted
1/2 t. salt
1/4 t. pepper
2-3 carrots, peeled and
shredded
1/2 cup minced onions
1/3 cup minced parsley
1/2 cup sour cream

Shred potatoes and place in ice water to cover. Stir together eggs, milk, flour, salt, and pepper. Drain potatoes and squeeze out any excess liquid. Add potatoes, carrots, onion, and parsley to egg mixture and stir together gently with a spoon. Drop by spoonfuls on lightly greased hot griddle and flatten each spoonful to a 4-inch circle. Turn when bottom is well browned. Serve with sour cream. *Makes about 14 pancakes.*

# SALADS

## PASTA SALAD

Cook the pasta in boiling water until tender; drain and rinse with cold water. Set aside. While the pasta is cooking, make the vinaigrette.

**Creamy Vinaigrette:** Place egg yolks in a blender and whirl until pale yellow. Add vinegar, mustard, and garlic. Whirl until blended. With blender running, add oil drop by drop until mixture thickens. Season with salt and pepper and refrigerate.

Cook broccoli, cauliflower, asparagus, snow peas, carrots, peppers, zucchini, and squash in boiling water until crisp-tender. Pour into a colander to drain. Immediately submerge in ice water to cool. Drain in a colander and set aside. Heat butter and oil in a small skillet until the butter is melted. Sauté mushrooms and then season with lemon pepper. In a large bowl, combine the cooked pasta, cooked vegetables, sautéed mushrooms, red onion, and cherry tomatoes. Pour on Creamy Vinaigrette dressing and then sprinkle on Parmesan cheese and parsley. Toss to combine. Refrigerate until ready to serve. *Serves 20.*

1-1/2 lbs. angel-hair pasta
1 lb. spinach tortellini
1 head broccoli, separated into flowerets
1 head cauliflower, separated into flowerets
1 lb. asparagus, tips only (reserve stalks for another use)
3/4 lb. snow peas
12 slender carrots, cut into julienne strips
3 small green bell peppers, cut into julienne strips
3 small red bell peppers, cut into julienne strips
2 slender zucchini, sliced diagonally
1 yellow squash, sliced diagonally
2 T. butter
2 T. olive oil
1 lb. mushrooms, sliced
generous amount of lemon pepper (or substitute the zest of 1 lemon)
1 red onion, thinly sliced
1/2 lb. cherry tomatoes, halved and seeded
1/3 cup grated Parmesan cheese
1/3 cup chopped fresh parsley

*Creamy Vinaigrette:*
5 egg yolks
1/2 cup tarragon cider vinegar
1 T. Dijon mustard
2 t. finely minced garlic
1-1/2 cups olive oil
salt and pepper

## SNOWPEA AND CARROT

2 cups fresh snowpeas, cut
  diagonally
2 carrots, cut in thin
  rounds

*Dressing:*
1 T. lemon juice
3 T. sesame oil
1 t. soy sauce
1 T. sunflower seeds
1/2 t. chopped mint

Simmer both vegetables in a little water until barely done. Add the dressing and serve hot or cold.

## SPINACH SALAD WITH BASIL, MUSHROOMS, AND GORGONZOLA CHEESE

1 lb. spinach, cleaned of
  stems, well washed and
  dried
3 ounces fresh basil
  leaves, washed and dried
6 large mushrooms,
  trimmed of woody stems
  and sliced
2 ounces imported
  Gorgonzola cheese,
  crumbled and well chilled
3/4 cup Mustard Vinaigrette

*Mustard Vinaigrette:*
4 ounces best quality olive
  oil
1 ounce red wine vinegar
1 ounce freshly squeezed
  lemon juice
1 T. finely chopped shallots
1 egg, beaten
1 t. Dijon mustard
generous amount of freshly
  ground black pepper

Fresh basil is essential to this salad. If you have no source for it, or wish to make it out of season, plant some basil seeds in a sunny window and use the sprouts. Since the sprouts don't have quite so strong a flavor, you may want to increase the amount.

Chilling the Gorgonzola maintains the flavor contrast. If you wish you can mix it into the vinaigrette.

Combine all ingredients with vinaigrette, toss well, and allow to sit for a few minutes to develop the flavor.

**Mustard Vinaigrette:** Combine all ingredients in a bowl and mix well. *Serves 4.*

# BUTTERMILK SALAD

In a blender, combine buttermilk, mustard, salt, pepper, lemon zest, and lemon juice. Blend until smooth and slowly add the olive oil. Add herb of choice and chill until ready to serve.

Peel carrots and cut in half lengthwise. Cut 1/2-inch slices on the diagonal. Bring a pot of water to a boil. Blanch the carrots until tender. Drain and dry in towels. Steam the potatoes until tender. Cool and cut into 1/2-inch wedges. Peel cucumbers and cut in quarters lengthwise. Seed cucumbers and cut into 1/2-inch slices on the diagonal. Trim and quarter radishes. Trim and slice scallions paper thin on the diagonal. Wash and dry lettuce leaves thoroughly. Arrange lettuce leaves on 6 plates. Toss carrots, potatoes, cucumbers, and radishes in a bowl. Pour some dressing over and toss to coat. Taste for salt and pepper and pile on lettuce leaves. Sprinkle top of salad with sliced scallions. Pass remaining dressing in a bowl.

1/2 cup buttermilk
2 T. prepared mustard
1/2 t. salt, or to taste
freshly ground black pepper
1 t. freshly grated lemon zest
few drops lemon juice
1-1/2 cups olive oil
2 T. freshly chopped parsley or dill
4 carrots
4 new potatoes
2 cucumbers
1 bunch radishes
2 scallions
6 lettuce leaves

# MARINATED MUSHROOMS AND GREEN BEANS

Combine dressing ingredients and mix well. Steam green beans until tender but not soft, then plunge into cold water. Mix beans with sliced mushrooms and scallions. Pour dressing over vegetables and allow to marinate about 2 hours. This is especially good as a salad combined with fresh raw spinach and croutons.

1/2 lb. fresh green beans, whole
2 cups sliced mushrooms
1 T. sliced scallions

*Dressing:*
2 cloves garlic, minced
1/2 t. salt
1/4 t. black pepper
1/4 t. finely grated lemon peel
1/4 cup fresh lemon juice
3/4 cup salad oil
1 T. chopped parsley
1/4 cup grated Parmesan cheese

## TOMATOES AND RIPE OLIVES IN CUMIN DRESSING

5 tomatoes, cut into slices
  or wedges
1 cup drained, pitted ripe
  olives
2 chopped onions
1/4 cup chopped parsley

*Dressing:*
1 t. salt
2 t. sugar
good dash of tumeric
1 scant t. ground cumin
1/4 t. freshly ground pepper
1/4 cup olive oil
4 T. lemon juice

Put all dressing ingredients in a small jar and shake to blend. Pour over vegetables in a shallow dish and refrigerate. Serve cold as is or on a bed of lettuce or a cushion of sprouts.

## TWO-CABBAGE SLAW

1/2 head green cabbage
1/2 head red cabbage
1/2 cup mayonnaise
2 T. lemon juice
2 T. cider vinegar
2 T. salad oil
2 T. sugar
2 T. horseradish
1 t. salt
1 t. celery seed
1/4 t. pepper

Shred cabbages thinly. Place in large bowl. In a quart jar, combine remaining ingredients and shake well. Pour over cabbage and toss to mix well. Cover bowl and let stand several hours so the flavors will blend. *Serves 6.*

## CRANBERRY SALAD

2 cups raw cranberries
1 orange, seeded
1 cup sugar
juice of 1/2 lemon
1 package lemon Jell-O
1 cup hot water
1 cup celery, minced
pinch of salt

Grind cranberries and orange, using a coarse blade. Add sugar and lemon juice and let mixture stand. Dissolve Jell-O in hot water and stir in cranberry mixture, celery, and salt. Pour into a 4-cup mold or bowl and chill. When firm, unmold if desired.

# BREADS & BREADSTUFFS

## ROSE'S BAGELS

In a large bowl mix together 1-1/2 cups flour, sugar, salt, and yeast. Gradually add egg yolk and warm water, and beat for 2 minutes at medium speed with an electric beater. Add 1/2 cup more flour and beat at high speed for 2 minutes. Add enough additional flour to make a soft dough. Turn dough onto a floured board. Knead for 8 to 10 minutes (add more flour if dough is too sticky). Place in an ungreased bowl. Cover, and let rise for 20 minutes (dough will not be doubled). Punch down and turn onto a floured board. Cut into about 10 pieces and roll each piece between your hands to make a rope; pinch the ends together to form circles. Place on ungreased baking sheets. Cover and let rise for 20 minutes (not until doubled). In a large shallow pan boil 1-3/4 inch water. Stir in honey. Lower heat and add a few bagels at a time. Simmer for 7 minutes. Place on a towel to cool for 5 minutes, then place on ungreased baking sheets. Bake bagels at 375°F. for 10 minutes. Remove from oven, brush with a mixture of egg white and water (and sprinkle with poppyseeds if desired), and return to oven. Bake for 20 minutes longer. Cool on wire racks. Serve split and toasted.

4 to 5 cups flour
3 T. sugar
1 T. salt
1 package yeast
1 egg yolk
1-1/2 cups very warm water
1 T. honey
1 egg white, beaten
1 T. cold water
poppyseeds (optional)

## FINNISH BRAID

5 to 5-1/2 cups flour
2 packages dry yeast (2 scant Tablespoons)
1/2 t. ground cardamom
1 cup milk
1/2 cup butter
1/2 cup sugar
1 t. salt
2 eggs
1 T. orange peel
1/3 cup orange juice
1 egg yolk
1 T. milk

In large bowl, mix 2 cups flour, yeast, and cardamom. In a saucepan, heat milk, butter, sugar, and salt to 120°F. to 130°F. Add to the dry mixture. Add eggs, peel, and juice. Beat at low speed for 30 seconds. Beat for 3 minutes at high speed. By hand, stir in 2 more cups flour. Turn onto a floured board and knead until smooth, adding more flour when necessary. Place dough in a greased bowl, and let rise, covered, until doubled. Punch down and divide in half. Divide each half into thirds; shape into six balls. Cover and let rise for 10 minutes. Roll each ball into a 16-inch rope. Braid three ropes together loosely and place on greased baking sheet, tucking ends under. Repeat with other braid. Cover and let rise until doubled. Brush with mixture of egg yolk and milk. Bake at 350°F. for 25 to 30 minutes. (Cover loosely with foil if loaves are browning too fast.)

## SWEDISH RYE BREAD

2 cups coarse rye flour
1 cup whole wheat flour
2/3 cup molasses
1/3 cup oil
2 t. salt
finely grated rind of 1 orange
juice of orange and enough boiling water to make 2 cups
1 package dry yeast (1 scant Tablespoon)
1/2 cup warm water
5 cups all-purpose flour

Combine rye flour, whole wheat flour, molasses, oil, salt, orange rind, and orange juice-water mixture in large bowl. Cool to lukewarm. Dissolve yeast in 1/2 cup warm water and add to mixture. Gradually add flour until dough is stiff. Kneading will be long and hard, but is worth the effort. Knead for 10 to 15 minutes, until dough is only slightly sticky. Place in greased bowl and let rise, covered, for about 2 hours. Punch down and allow to rise again for 30 minutes. Shape into three oblong loaves and let rise about 1 hour. Bake at 350°F. for 30 to 40 minutes, or until done.

# QUICK COTTAGE CHEESE DILL BREAD

In a large bowl mix the flour, baking powder, baking soda, salt, and dill. In a small saucepan combine the oil and honey and heat until just blended. Remove from heat and stir in the milk, beaten egg, and cottage cheese. Pour this mixture into the flour mixture and beat just until combined. Do not overbeat. Scrape into a buttered and floured loaf pan and press down the batter with a rubber spatula to prevent any air pockets from forming. Smooth over the top, then give the pan a good thump on your counter. Bake at 375°F. for 45 to 50 minutes, until golden. Cool for 10 minutes on a wire rack, then remove bread from pan and continue cooling for an hour before slicing. *Makes 1 loaf.*

2-1/2 cups whole wheat pastry flour (or 1-1/4 cups whole wheat flour and 1-1/4 cups unbleached white flour)
2 t. baking powder
1/2 t. baking soda
3/4 t. salt
2 heaping tablespoons minced fresh dill
1/4 cup oil
1/4 cup honey
3/4 cup milk
1 egg, well beaten
1 cup cottage cheese

# ANNE'S BREAD

Heat milk, butter, salt, and 6 tablespoons sugar together to scald, and cool to lukewarm. Mix together warm water, 1 tablespoon sugar, and yeast, and allow to proof. Add yeast to milk in large bowl, and mix in grains, adding enough white flour to make a smooth dough. Knead well (10 to 15 minutes) and let rise until doubled in a greased bowl. Punch down, shape into loaves, and let rise again until nearly doubled. Bake for about 1 hour at 350°F. *Makes 6 loaves.*

6 cups milk (can use part yogurt, sour milk, buttermilk, etc.)
1 stick butter or margarine
1 T. salt
6 T. sugar
3/4 cup warm water
1 T. sugar
3 packages dry yeast
1 to 2 cups soy flour
2/3 cup unprocessed bran
1/3 cup wheat germ
1-1/2 cups whole wheat flour
1 handful each: cornmeal, oatmeal
2 handfuls of your favorite wheat cereal, crushed
4 cups or more unbleached white flour

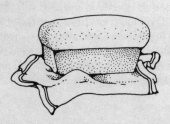

# ZUCCHINI FRENCH BREAD

1 t. dry yeast
1/2 cup unbleached flour
1/2 cup water
1 to 2 cups puréed zucchini
1 t. salt
4 to 6 cups unbleached
  flour

Mix yeast, 1/2 cup flour, and water together in a bowl to make a sponge and set in a warm place for two hours. Using a food processor or a large bowl, combine sponge with remaining ingredients, using enough flour to make a soft dough. Knead by hand or process until smooth and satiny. Cover and let rise until double. Form into long loaves and place in greased oblong pans. Let rest for 5 minutes, then slash diagonally with a razor. Place in a cold oven set at 400°F.; bake for about 40 minutes.

# MUFFINS AND VARIATIONS

2 cups flour
1 T. baking powder
3/4 t. salt
1/2 cup sugar
1 egg, lightly beaten
1 cup milk
3 T. melted shortening

Combine dry ingredients. Combine egg, milk, and melted shortening, and pour into flour mixture. Stir enough to moisten dry ingredients, but do not beat. Fill greased muffin tins 2/3 full. Bake for 20 to 25 minutes at 400°F.

**Bacon or Sausage Muffins:** add 1/2 cup crisp bacon, crumbled, to dry ingredients, or add 1/2 cup cooked sausage, well drained.

**Blueberry or Apple Muffins:** Add 1 cup blueberries or 1 cup chopped apples, and 1 to 2 extra tablespoons flour to dry mixture.

**Cheese Muffins:** Add 1 cup grated Cheddar cheese to dry mixture.

# MARIANNA ESSEX'S BLUEBERRY MUFFINS

2 cups unbleached flour
1/2 t. salt
3 t. baking powder
2 T. sugar
3/4 cup milk
1 beaten egg
3 T. melted butter
1 cup blueberries, fresh or
  thawed

Preheat oven to 400°F. to 425°F. Sift dry ingredients. Mix milk, egg, and shortening and add to dry ingredients. Stir until moistened but not smooth. Batter should be lumpy. Add blueberries. Fill greased muffin tins 2/3 full and bake 20 to 25 minutes. *Makes 12 muffins.*

## REFRIGERATOR BRAN MUFFINS

Pour boiling water over first 2 cups of bran; add raisins, stir, and set aside. In large bowl, cream sugar, honey, and shortening. Add eggs and beat well. Blend in buttermilk. Add bran and raisin mixture. Add the 4 cups bran and mix. Sift flour with soda and salt. Add to bran mixture and mix well. Cover tightly and store in refrigerator. This will keep for 6 weeks. To bake muffins, merely spoon into greased muffin tins without stirring and bake 16 to 20 minutes at 400°F.

2 cups boiling water
2 cups All-Bran
1 cup raisins
2 cups sugar
1/2 cup honey
1 cup plus 3 T. shortening
4 eggs
1 quart buttermilk
4 cups All-Bran
6 cups flour
5 t. baking soda
2 t. salt

## MAPLE OATMEAL MUFFINS

Stir together egg, milk, shortening, and maple sugar. Mix flour, baking powder, and salt together and add to egg mixture. Stir in rolled oats until just blended. Add raisins if desired. spoon into greased muffin tins and bake at 400°F. to 425°F. for 15 to 20 minutes. *Makes 12 large muffins.*

1 egg, beaten
1 cup milk
1/4 cup melted shortening
3/4 cup soft maple sugar
1-1/2 cups flour
1 T. baking powder
3/4 t. salt
1-1/4 cups rolled oats
1/4 to 1/2 cup raisins, if
   desired

## JEAN BOARDMAN'S APPLE MUFFINS

Peel and dice apples. Beat together egg, milk, and oil. Add flour, sugar, cinnamon, baking powder, and salt. Stir in apples. Fill greased muffin tins 2/3 full and bake at 400°F. for 20 to 30 minutes.

3 apples
1 egg
1/2 cup milk
1/4 cup oil
1-1/2 cups flour
1/2 cup sugar
1 t. cinnamon
2 t. baking powder
1/2 t. salt

## RAISIN AND COTTAGE CHEESE BUNS

1 cup cottage cheese
3 T. milk
1 egg, separated
1/3 cup oil
1/3 cup sugar
1 cup whole wheat flour
1/2 cup white flour
2 t. baking powder
1/2 cup raisins
1/2 cup chopped nuts
5 T. sugar
1 T. cinnamon

Mix together cottage cheese, milk, egg yolk (reserve egg white), oil, and sugar. Mix flours and baking powder together and add to cottage cheese mixture. Knead for only a short time and roll into an 8" by 17" rectangle. Baste with the egg white. Sprinkle with raisins, nuts, sugar, and cinnamon. Roll up to make a long cylinder and cut into 12 pieces. Place in greased pan and bake in 350°F. oven for about 25 minutes. *Makes 12.*

## GINGERED BISCUITS

4 cups flour
2 T baking powder
2 t. salt
1/2 cup shortening
1 cup candied ginger,
  grated
1-1/2 cups milk
1 egg white plus 1 T. water

Combine flour, baking powder, and salt in a bowl. Add shortening and cut in until mixture resembles crumbs. Stir in all but 2 tablespoons of the grated ginger. Gradually stir in milk until dough sticks together. Knead briefly. Roll to 1/2-inch thickness and cut into 2-inch rounds. Transfer to an ungreased baking sheet. Whisk together egg white and water. Brush over the tops of the biscuits and then sprinkle on the remaining grated ginger. Bake at 450°F. for 12 to 15 minutes. *Makes 24.*

## MAPLE SUGAR BISCUITS

2 cups flour
3 t. baking powder
1/2 t. salt
1/4 cup shortening
3/4 cup milk
2-3 T. melted butter
1/2 cup crushed maple
  sugar

Sift dry ingredients into a bowl. Cut in shortening. Add milk to make soft dough. Place on floured board and toss lightly. Roll out 1/2-inch thick and cut with floured biscuit cutter. Place on greased cookie sheet. Brush tops of biscuits with melted butter and sprinkle with maple sugar. Bake at 450°F. for about 10 to 12 minutes. *Makes 12.*

## SHAKER RAISED SQUASH BISCUITS

In a small saucepan heat milk and butter to very hot. Mix sugar and salt in large bowl and pour in milk. Let sugar/milk mixture cool until lukewarm. Add yeast and 2 cups flour. Beat at medium speed in a mixer for 2 minutes. Add squash and eggs. Mix well. Continue to add flour (with wooden spoon) until you have a stiff dough; the dough should begin to leave the sides of the bowl. Turn out onto a floured board and knead 7 to 8 minutes, using additional flour on the board to prevent sticking. Put back in clean, greased bowl. Turn dough greased side up and cover with a towel. Let rise in a warm place until double. Punch dough down and turn out. Shape into biscuits. Place in square 8" by 8" pan for soft sides, in muffin pans, or shape into cloverleaf rolls. Let rise double again. Bake in a preheated 400°F. oven until brown, about 25 minutes. Butter tops while hot. *Makes 2-1/2 to 3 dozen.*

1 cup milk
4 T. butter or margarine
3/4 cup sugar
1/2 t. salt
1 yeast cake, or 1 envelope (1 scant tablespoon) dry yeast
4 to 5 cups flour
1-1/2 cups butternut squash, strained (or 1 16-ounce can of squash)
2 eggs, at room temperature

## EMPIRE BISCUITS

Sift and mix together all the dry ingredients. Rub butter into the mixture. Add the beaten egg, lemon juice, and almond extract to make a stiff paste. Roll between two sheets of waxed paper and cut with a cookie cutter. Bake in a 375°F. oven 10 to 15 minutes, depending on thickness. When cool, store in a tin. These keep indefinitely. For variety put two biscuits together with jam, ice the top with boiled white icing, and crown it with a cherry.

4 cups flour
1 cup sugar
2 t. baking powder
1/4 t. cinnamon
1/2 t. salt
1/2 lb. butter
1 egg, beaten
1 T. lemon juice
1/2 t. almond extract

# DESSERTS

## CHILLED CHOCOLATE LOAF *(Dolce Torinese)*

1/2 lb. semi-sweet
  chocolate
1/4 cup rum
1/2 lb. unsalted butter
2 T. superfine sugar
2 eggs, separated
1-1/2 cups ground
  blanched almonds
pinch of salt
12 butter biscuits (Social
  Teas or Petite Buerre
  biscuits)
confectioner's sugar
1/2 cup heavy cream,
  whipped

Lightly grease bottom and sides of 1-1/2 quart loaf pan with vegetable oil; invert pan to drain excess. In a heavy pan melt chocolate over low heat, stirring constantly to prevent scorching. When melted, stir in rum and remove from heat to cool. Cream butter until fluffy. Beat in sugar, then egg yolks one at a time. Stir in almonds and melted chocolate. Beat egg whites and salt until soft peaks form. Fold into the chocolate mixture until no whites show. Cut the biscuits into 1" by 1/2" pieces, discarding crumbs; fold into chocolate mixture. Spoon into the greased pan and smooth the top. Cover with plastic and chill for at least 4 hours. Unmold 1 hour before serving by running a thin knife around the edges and dipping pan briefly in hot water before inverting onto a platter. Smooth the sides. Dust with confectioner's sugar (shake it through a sieve). Serve in thin slices with whipped cream.

## CHEESECAKE

6 eggs, separated
3/4 cup sugar
1/2 cup cake flour
1/2 lb. cream cheese
1/2 lb. farmer cheese (dry
  cottage cheese)
1 pint sour cream
1 t. lemon juice
1 graham-cracker crust in
  spring-form pan

Beat egg whites with 1/4 cup sugar and set aside. In large bowl combine remaining sugar, flour, cheeses, sour cream, and lemon juice. Beat until very smooth, about 10 minutes. Fold in whites and pour mixture into crust. Bake at 325°F. for 1 hour. Turn off oven, open oven door, and let cheesecake cool in oven.

## CHEESECAKE SQUARES

Combine flour and brown sugar; cut in butter until mixture is crumbly. Keep out 1 cup of mixture and press the remainder into an ungreased 8" by 8" pan. Bake at 350°F. for 12 to 15 minutes. Meanwhile, combine cream cheese, sugar, egg, milk, and lemon rind and juice and beat well. Spread over baked crust. Combine 1 cup reserved topping with chopped nuts, and sprinkle over cheese mixture. Bake at 350°F. for 25 minutes. Cool and cut into squares.

1 cup flour
1/2 cup brown sugar
6 T. butter
8 ounces cream cheese, softened
1/4 cup sugar
1 egg
2 T. milk
1/4 t. lemon rind
2 T. lemon juice
2 T. chopped nuts

## PECAN COCONUT CAKE

Mix together the butter, sugar, eggs, vanilla and coconut until well blended. Sift together flour, baking powder, and salt, and add this to first mixture, alternately with milk and beat until smooth. Mix the pecans into the batter. Pour into greased 8" by 8" pan.

**Topping:** Mix all ingredients together and sprinkle over top of mixture. Bake 375°F. for 30 minutes.

1/3 cup butter or margarine
1 cup brown sugar, firmly packed
2 eggs, unbeaten
1-1/2 t. vanilla
1/3 cup coconut
1-1/2 cups sifted all-purpose flour
1-1/2 t. baking powder
1/2 t. salt
1/3 cup milk
1/2 cup pecan nuts

*Topping:*
1/2 cup all-purpose flour
1/2 cup brown sugar
1/4 cup hard butter or margarine
1/2 cup pecan nuts
1/3 cup coconut

## CREAM PUFFS

1 stick butter
1 cup water
1 cup flour
dash of salt
4 eggs

*Cream Puff Filling:*
1/2 cup sugar
5 T. flour
1/8 t. salt
1/4 cup cold milk
1-1/2 cups scalded milk
3 egg yolks
3 egg whites, stiffly beaten
1 t. vanilla

Put butter and water in a saucepan. Place over low heat until mixture boils. Add flour and salt all at once and cook until thick and smooth, stirring constantly. Remove from heat and add unbeaten eggs one at a time, mixing throughly after each addition. Place dough in mounds about 1-1/2 inches apart on a greased baking sheet and bake at 400°F. about 35 minutes, until puffed and golden. To fill, cut horizontally with a sharp knife. Fill with Cream Puff Filling or with whipped cream.

**Cream Puff Filling:** Mix sugar, flour, and salt together with cold milk and pour slowly into scalded milk. Add egg yolks and cook in a double boiler until thickened. Fold in stiffly beaten egg whites. Cool and add vanilla.

## GRAM WHITE'S SOFT GINGER COOKIES

2/3 cup cooking oil
1 cup sugar
1 cup molasses
1 medium egg, well beaten
3 t. soda dissolved in 1/2
   cup boiling water

*Sift together:*
5-1/2 cups all-purpose flour
3 t. cream of tartar
1 t. ginger
1 t. cinnamon
1/2 t. salt

Beat together the oil and sugar, add molasses and mix well. Add egg and mix. Add boiling water and soda. Add dry ingredients, mix well. Chill, overnight if convenient. Roll out 1/4-inch thick on a floured and sugared surface. Cut cookies and bake on a greased cookie sheet for 8 to 10 minutes in a 400°F. oven. Watch carefully. (This recipe is at least 150 years old.)

## BISCOTTI *(Italian Cookies)*

Add flour mixture to other ingredients and beat until smooth and satiny. If too soft, work in more flour. Roll into little loaves (3" by 1"). Place on greased cookie sheet. Bake at 350°F. until brown (about 15 to 20 minutes). When cool, slice into 1/2-inch slices. Arrange slices on baking sheet and return to oven to dry out (about 10 minutes longer). Cool, put in covered container. *Makes 6 dozen cookies.*

*Measure and sift together the following ingredients:*
2 cups sifted flour
2 t. baking powder
1/2 t. salt

*Combine:*
3 well-beaten eggs
1 cup sugar
1/2 cup margarine, melted
2 t. vanilla
1 T. anise extract
1 cup chopped walnuts

## RHUBARB CRUNCH

**Crust:** Mix oatmeal, brown sugar, salt, flour, and butter together. Press half of it on the bottom of a 9" by 13" pan.

**Filling:** Spread diced rhubarb on top of crust. Boil sugar, water, and cornstarch until thick. Add almond flavoring. Add pie filling and spoon mixture over rhubarb. Sprinkle the remaining crust mixture over the top. Then the nuts. Bake 45 minutes at 350°F. Serve with whipped cream or dairy substitute.

*Crust:*
1 cup quick oatmeal
1 cup brown sugar
1 cup flour and a pinch of salt
1/2 cup butter

*Filling:*
4 cups diced fresh rhubarb
1 cup sugar
1 cup water
2 T. cornstarch
1 t. almond flavoring
1 can cherry pie filling mix
1/2 cup chopped nuts

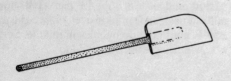

## STRAWBERRY PIE PLATTER

pastry for single-crust pie
1 qt. fresh strawberries,
  cleaned and hulled
2 T. sugar

*Orange Sauce:*
1 cup sugar
1/4 t. salt
2 T. cornstarch
1 cup orange juice
1/4 cup lemon juice
3/4 cup water

Roll pastry into a 10-inch circle. Place on pizza pan and flute edge after folding in 1/2 inch. Prick pastry all over with a fork and bake at 400°F. for about 10 to 15 minutes or until lightly browned. Set aside to cool. Place strawberries, stem end down, in circles on the crust. Brush with Orange Sauce and sprinkle with sugar. Cut pie into wedges and serve with orange sauce and whipped cream.

**Orange Sauce:** In a small saucepan, mix sugar, salt, and cornstarch. Stir in juices and water. Cook, stirring constantly, until mixture boils and thickens. Boil 1 minute. Cool.

## STRAWBERRY-RHUBARB PIE

1 cup sugar
1 T. cornstarch
1 t. minute tapioca
1/8 t. salt
pastry for double-crust pie
2 cups strawberries
1 cup rhubarb, cut in
  1/4-inch slices
1 T. butter

Mix sugar, cornstarch, tapioca, and salt together. Line a 9-inch pie plate with pastry. Mix strawberries, rhubarb, and sugar mixture together and place in pie pan. Dot with butter and cover with top crust. Bake in very hot oven (450°F.) for 10 minutes; reduce heat to 350°F. and bake about 30 minutes longer.

## APPLE GOODY

1/2 of #10 can sliced apples
  (use a hard pie apple,
  such as New York
  Greening), or 3 20-ounce
  cans
1 cup dark brown sugar
flour
1/2 lb. butter
2 cups oatmeal

Mix together apples and sugar with a dusting of flour, and place in 9" by 13" pan. Melt butter, add oatmeal, and sprinkle over apples. Bake at 350°F. until mixture bubbles in middle. Serve hot, with ice cream. *Serves 10 to 12.*

## APPLE-CRUMB PIE

Mix apple slices with 1/2 cup sugar and cinnamon and sprinkle with lemon juice. Pile the apple slices into an unbaked pie shell. Mix 1/3 cup sugar and flour together and cut in butter until the mixture is crumbly. Sprinkle the crumb mixture over the apples. Bake 35 to 45 minutes at 400°F. If crumb crust is becoming too brown, protect with foil covering until apples are tender.

5 cups apples, sliced
1/2 cup sugar
3/4 t. cinnamon
2 to 3 T. lemon juice,
  according to sweetness
  of apples
unbaked pie shell
1/3 cup sugar
3/4 cup flour
6 T. butter

## LEMON-ORANGE MOUSSE

Dissolve gelatin in juice and rind of orange and lemon. Whip the cream and add confectioner's sugar. Add the gelatin mixture slowly, stirring constantly. Spoon into serving glasses and chill. *Serves 4.*

1/2 T. gelatin
juice and rind of 1 orange
juice and rind of 1 lemon
2 cups whipping cream
1/2 cup confectioner's
  sugar

## CARAMEL CRÈME WITH FRESH RASPBERRIES

Heat the sugar in a heavy pan until golden and bubbly, being careful not to burn it. Remove the pan from the heat and add hot milk, stirring until the sugar is dissolved. (Return pan to the heat if necessary.) Beat the egg yolks and add the cornstarch. Add a bit of the hot milk to the eggs and then slowly add the eggs to the rest of the hot milk. Cook over low heat, stirring constantly, until mixture thickens and bubbles for 1 minute. Cool. Stir in brandy and chill. Fold in whipped cream just before serving. Fill 6 glasses 2/3 full and fill to the top with raspberries.

1/2 cup sugar
2 cups hot milk
4 egg yolks
3 T. cornstarch
1 to 2 T. brandy
1 cup whipped cream
2 cups fresh raspberries

## CHOCOLATE CARAMELS

1-1/3 cups (15-ounce can) sweetened condensed milk
1 cup light corn syrup
1 T. butter
1/8 t. salt
2 squares (2-ounce) unsweetened chocolate
1 t. vanilla extract

In 1-1/2 quart heavy saucepan mix together 1/3 cup condensed milk, corn syrup, butter, and salt. Cook over medium heat, stirring constantly, to 235°F. or until a little when dropped in cold water forms a ball. Stir in remaining cup of milk. Stir in chocolate, a piece at a time. Boil until syrup temperature reaches 235°F. again. Remove. Stir in vanilla extract. Pour into 8" by 8" by 2" buttered pan. Cool. Cut into 1/2-inch squares. *Makes 1 pound.*

## PEPPERMINT-CHOCOLATE ICE CREAM

1-1/2 cups raw milk or light cream, scalded
1/2 t. peppermint extract
1-1/2 cups finely crushed peppermint candies
2 T. flour
pinch of salt
2 eggs, room temperature
1-1/2 cups heavy cream, partially beaten
12 ounces chocolate or carob bits

Mix milk, extract, and 1 cup of the candies (reserving 1/2 cup) together, and scald in a double boiler. Mix flour and salt and stir in enough milk to make a smooth paste. Stir into rest of milk in double boiler and continue cooking, stirring until thickened. Then cook, covered, for 10 minutes. Beat the eggs and stir into the milk mixture. Return to the double boiler and cook for 1 minute. Cool. Add cream and freeze in a hand freezer. After 5 minutes of churning, add the 1/2 cup of peppermints and the chocolate bits, then complete the freezing process. Pack and let ripen for 2 hours. *Makes 1/2 gallon.*

## CIDER SHERBET

4 cups fresh-pressed cider
1/2 cup sugar
1 cup fresh-squeezed orange juice
juice of 2 lemons

Simmer the cider and sugar together for 5 minutes. Cool. Add juices and freeze in hand freezer, using equal parts salt and ice. Eat right away. *Makes 1/2 gallon.*

# QUICHE

## PROVIDENCE CHEESE QUICHE

This crustless quiche is delicious, nutritious, and easy to make, and with no crust, lighter than most. It will make 8 moderate-sized servings and can be made in a round pan if you prefer. Preheat oven to 350°F. Beat ricotta and eggs together well until creamy and light in color. Add salt and pepper, Parmesan cheese, and spinach. Blend thoroughly and pour mixture into a lightly oiled 8" by 8" by 2" baking pan. Sprinkle top with bread crumbs and bake approximately 15 minutes, or until golden.

Raw, finely diced or grated zucchini may be used instead of the spinach.
1-1/2 lbs. fresh, well-drained ricotta cheese
4 eggs, well beaten
salt and pepper to taste
2 T. grated Parmesan cheese
2 cups raw spinach, chopped
1/4 cup freshly grated bread crumbs

## QUICHE LORRAINE

Chop onion in food processor and sauté in butter until transparent. Cook bacon, drain, and crumble. Add to onions. Beat eggs until light and foamy. Add crème fraîche and seasonings to eggs and blend well. Place onion-bacon mixture in pie shell. Top with grated cheese. Pour egg mixture over cheese and sprinkle with nutmeg. Bake at 375°F. for 30 to 35 minutes, until golden brown. Insert knife into quiche. If it comes out clean, the quiche is cooked. *Serves 6 to 8.*

1 10-inch pie shell, unbaked
1 onion
1 T. butter
1 lb. bacon
5 eggs plus 1 egg yolk
2-1/2 cups crème fraîche
1/8 t. salt
2 dashes cayenne pepper
1 dash white pepper
1 cup Gruyère or Comte cheese, grated
grating of fresh nutmeg

## LEEK AND HERB QUICHE

1 unbaked pie shell (use favorite pie crust recipe)
3/4 cup grated Swiss cheese
2 cups sliced leeks (use only white section)
2 T. butter
2 cups heavy cream
2-1/2 cups light cream
1 t. salt
1/4 t. white pepper
1/2 t. dill
pinch of thyme
1 T. chopped fresh parsley
1 clove garlic, minced
5 eggs, beaten

Sprinkle cheese on bottom of pie shell. Sauté leeks in butter until soft. Layer leeks evenly over cheese. In saucepan, bring creams and seasonings to boil. Beat eggs and mix in hot cream, beating constantly. Pour mixture into pie shell. Bake at 375°F. for 40 minutes, or until a knife inserted into the center comes out clean.

Cooked vegetables, seafood, or meat may be used in place of or in addition to the leeks.

## JUDY EGGLESTON'S TURKEY-BROCCOLI QUICHE

pastry for one 10-inch pie shell or quiche pan
1 cup shredded Swiss or Grùyere cheese
1/2 cup chopped scallions
1 cup broccoli, cooked but still crisp
1-1/2 cups cooked turkey white meat, diced
4 eggs
1-1/2 cups half-and-half cream
1 t. salt
1/4 t. pepper
1/2 t. ground nutmeg

Preheat oven to 375°F. and bake pie shell for 10 minutes. Let cool. Line the shell with shredded cheese, reserving a portion for the topping. Layer in scallions, broccoli, and turkey. Beat the eggs and cream together and add seasonings. Pour the mixture over the turkey and broccoli and sprinkle remaining cheese over the top. Bake for 45 minutes at 375°F., until a knife inserted in the center comes out clean. *Serves 6.*

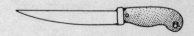

## LOBSTER QUICHE

Preheat oven to 425°F. Sprinkle lobster, cheese, and onion into shell. Beat eggs. Pour cream into eggs and add seasonings and parsley flakes. Pour into shell. Bake for 15 minutes at 425°F., then reduce heat to 300°F. Bake 35 to 45 minutes or until knife comes out clean when inserted one inch from the edge. Let quiche stand 10 minutes before serving.

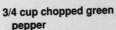

1 9 inch unbaked pastry shell
1 cup lobster meat
1 cup shredded Swiss cheese
1/3 cup minced onion
4 eggs
2 cups light cream
1/2 t. salt
1/8 t. cayenne pepper
dash of parsley flakes

## SPINACH QUICHE

Sauté peppers, onion, celery, zucchini, and garlic in hot oil. Beat eggs and combine with cream cheese, Cheddar cheese, and seasonings. Add spinach and Parmesan cheese to egg mixture and combine with vegetables. Mix well. Bake in a 10-inch springform pan (or make two thin pies by using two pans) at 350°F. for 1 hour, until pie is set in center. Cool 10 minutes before cutting.

3/4 cup chopped green pepper
3/4 cup chopped onion
1-1/2 cups chopped celery (can substitute mushrooms)
2 cups chopped zucchini
1-1/2 t. minced garlic
3 T. oil
7 eggs
1 8-ounce package cream cheese, softened and diced
3 cups Cheddar cheese, shredded
1 t. seasoned salt
1/8 t. pepper
basil to taste
2 10-ounce packages chopped spinach, cooked and drained
1 to 1-1/2 cups grated Parmesan cheese

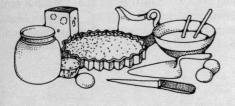

# SAUCES

### NEWBURG SAUCE

2 T. butter
Spanish paprika (not as
    dark as other paprika)
3 T. flour
2 cups milk
1 to 2 T. sherry (preferably
    Harvey's Bristol Cream)

Melt butter and add enough Spanish paprika to make a bright red liquid. Add enough flour to make a roux. Scald milk, and thicken with roux. Season, and add sherry to taste. Let come to a bubble and cook gently so sherry won't taste raw. Strain to make smooth. Makes 2 cups. This sauce can be held warm on the side by putting a little butter on top so a skin won't form. Use on fish and chicken. Add 1/2 pound shrimp and serve hot over 3 to 4 pounds fresh baked scrod.

### QUICK MINT SAUCE

1-1/2 T. confectioner's
    sugar
3 T. hot water
1/2 cup vinegar
1/3 cup chopped fresh mint
    leaves

Dissolve confectioner's sugar in hot water. Let cool. Add vinegar and chopped fresh mint leaves.

### TOMATO SAUCE

1/4 onion, chopped
1 garlic clove, chopped
pinch of red pepper flakes
bay leaves
dash of oregano
2 T. oil
1 medium can of tomato
    paste
1 can of tomatoes (large
    kitchen-ready)
salt and pepper to taste
1/4 to 1/2 t. basil

Sauté onion, garlic, and spices in oil until transparent. Add tomato paste and stir until well blended. Add tomatoes and stir well. Add tomato can of water. Let mixture come to full boil and add salt, pepper, and basil leaves.

GARLIC

# SALAD DRESSING

## HERBED VINAIGRETTE SAUCE FOR SALAD

The combination of garlic, wine vinegar, and tarragon makes an excellent zesty dressing for greens of all sorts, but particularly for Boston lettuce.

Combine olive oil with seasonings and gradually beat in the vinegar, tasting as you add to determine proper proportions. Wash and dry lettuce. Toss lettuce with dressing and sprinkle on croutons. *Makes about 3/4 cup.*

1/2 cup olive oil
1/2 t. salt
1 clove garlic, put through press
1 t. Dijon mustard
1 t. tarragon (optional)
1 t. parsley
2-3 T. wine vinegar or lemon juice
Boston lettuce, torn into bite-size pieces
1/2 cup croutons, more or less

## HONEY DRESSING

Beat first three ingredients together, then add honey slowly while beating.

1/3 cup oil
2-1/2 T. lemon juice
1/2 t. salt
1/3 cup strained honey

## CREAMY FRENCH DRESSING

Combine the first 6 ingredients and let stand for an hour. Add remaining ingredients. Beat vigorously with a rotary egg beater. *Makes 3 cups.*

2 cups salad oil
1 clove garlic
2 t. grated onion
1/2 t. powdered dry mustard
1/8 t. ground black pepper
1 t. paprika
1 t. salt
1/4 cup catsup
2 T. sugar
3/4 cup cider vinegar
1 egg white

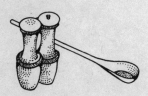

## HOT BACON DRESSING

2 slices bacon, cut in small
pieces
2 T. sugar
2 T. ketchup
1 T. chopped onion
1 T. red-wine vinegar
1 T. Worcestershire sauce

Cook bacon until crisp and remove from pan with slotted spoon. Add sugar, ketchup, onion, vinegar, and Worcestershire sauce to bacon grease in the pan. Bring to a boil and reduce slightly. Add bacon; pour over prepared salad and serve at once.

## HONEY AND BASIL VINEGAR SALAD DRESSING

1/2 cup honey
3/4 cup olive oil
1/2 cup basil vinegar
1 clove garlic
1/2 cup fresh basil
dash of salt

Mix all in a blender and store in the refrigerator. May be poured over sliced tomatoes or salad greens.

## ROQUEFORT CHEESE DRESSING

1 cup Roquefort cheese
1 cup whipped cream
1 cup salad oil
1 cup vinegar
1 t. salt
1 t. paprika
few grains cayenne pepper

Let cheese stand at room temperature until it softens, then mash with a fork. Beat until smooth, then add remaining ingredients.

# RELISH

## PEARLE GOODWIN'S CRANBERRY MAPLE RELISH

Pick over and wash cranberries and put them through a food chopper. Wash, but do not peel, the oranges and lemon. Cut them into chunks, remove seeds, and put through the fine knife of a food chopper. Add to chopped cranberries and chill. Place sugar and syrup over medium low heat in large pan. Add ginger and stir constantly until brought to a rolling boil. Remove from heat, cool, and add to fruit. Stir well, then place in sterile jars. Will keep in refrigerator for several weeks. Serve with roast poultry.

1 lb. fresh raw cranberries
2 small sweet oranges
1 large lemon
1-1/2 cups maple syrup
1 cup dark brown sugar
1/2 t. ground ginger

## CURRIED APPLE RELISH

Melt butter in skillet. Stir in sugar and curry. Add apples and toss together. Cook over low heat until apples are heated through. Serve with poultry or meat.

2 T. butter
1 t. sugar (white or brown)
1/2 t. curry powder
1 1-lb. 4-ounce can (2-1/2 cups) pie-sliced apples, drained

## COPLEY PLAZA RELISH

Put green tomatoes through the food chopper. Add salt and let stand overnight. Drain green tomatoes and add other ingredients. Cook about 30 minutes. Put in sterilized jars and seal.

1 quart green tomatoes
1/2 cup salt
1 quart ripe tomatoes, cut fine
2 green peppers, seeded and chopped
3 red peppers, seeded and chopped
5 small onions, chopped
1 pint vinegar
3 cups sugar

# JAMS, JELLIES & MARMALADES

## CURRANT AND RASPBERRY JELLY

3-1/2 lbs. raspberries and
  currants in equal
  amounts
sugar

Wash fruit, leaving stems on currants. Crush fruit thoroughly. Bring fruit slowly just to the boiling point, stirring constantly. Strain through three thicknesses of cheesecloth or any other thin material. Give it plenty of time to drip.

Measure juice and place it in a large pan with two-thirds as much sugar as there is juice. Boil rapidly until mixture jells (222° F. if tested with a candy thermometer). The spoon test can be used: dip spoon into juice; if it sheets from the spoon or two drops hang together from the side the jelly is done.

## TAIYA'S BLUEBERRY-RASPBERRY JAM

4 cups raspberries
4 cups blueberries
7 cups sugar
1 bottle pectin

Crush the berries with a wooden spoon, add sugar, mix well. Heat to full rolling boil and boil for one minute, stirring constantly. Remove from heat, add pectin, skim the top and pour into sterilized jars. Seal with paraffin. *Makes 11 6-ounce glasses of jam.*

## PEACH MARMALADE

firm but ripe peaches
sugar
oranges

Peel and slice peaches. For each cup of fruit add one cup of sugar. For every 5 cups of fruit add one orange, seeded and minced or cut in very thin slices.

Let these ingredients stand for 2 hours. Then boil them, stirring frequently until the syrup is quite thick.